AQA GCSE Mathematics

FOUNDATION TIER

Series Editor | Trevor Senior

Linear Course

Homework Book

Published by: Pearson Education Limited, Edinburgh Gate, Harlow, Essex, CM20 2JE, England
www.longman.co.uk

First published 2007

ISBN: 978-1-4058-1581-9
Cover design by Juice Creative Ltd.

Typeset by Tech-Set, Gateshead

Printed in Malaysia, KHL

The publisher's policy is to use paper manufactured from sustainable forests.

Contents

1 Working with numbers   **1**
1.1 Exercise A   1
1.1 Exercise B   1
1.2 Exercise A   1
1.2 Exercise B   2
1.3 Exercise A   2
1.3 Exercise B   3
1.4 Exercise A   3
1.4 Exercise B   4
1.5 Exercise A   4
1.5 Exercise B   5
1.6 Exercise A   5
1.6 Exercise B   6

2 Angles in shapes   **6**
2.1 Exercise A   6
2.1 Exercise B   7
2.2 Exercise A   7
2.2 Exercise B   8
2.3 Exercise A   8
2.3 Exercise B   8
2.4 Exercise A   9
2.4 Exercise B   9

3 Powers and roots   **10**
3.1 Exercise A   10
3.1 Exercise B   10
3.2 Exercise A   10
3.2 Exercise B   10
3.3 Exercise A   10
3.3 Exercise B   11

4 Collecting data   **11**
4.1 Exercise A   11
4.1 Exercise B   12
4.2 Exercise A   12
4.2 Exercise B   12
4.3 Exercise A   12
4.3 Exercise B   13

5 Operations   **13**
5.1 Exercise A   13
5.1 Exercise B   14
5.2 Exercise A   14
5.2 Exercise B   14
5.3 Exercise A   14
5.3 Exercise B   15
5.4 Exercise A   15
5.4 Exercise B   16

6 Introducing algebra   **16**
6.1 Exercise A   16
6.1 Exercise B   16
6.2 Exercise A   17
6.2 Exercise B   17
6.3 Exercise A   17
6.3 Exercise B   18
6.4 Exercise A   18
6.4 Exercise B   18

7 Multiples, factors and primes   **18**
7.1 Exercise A   18
7.1 Exercise B   19
7.2 Exercise A   19
7.2 Exercise B   19
7.3 Exercise A   19
7.3 Exercise B   20
7.4 Exercise A   20
7.4 Exercise B   20

8 Measures   **20**
8.1 Exercise A   20
8.1 Exercise B   21
8.2 Exercise A   21
8.2 Exercise B   21
8.3 Exercise A   22
8.3 Exercise B   22

9 Equations   **23**
9.1 Exercise A   23
9.1 Exercise B   23
9.2 Exercise A   23
9.2 Exercise B   24

10 Fractions, decimals and percentages   **24**
10.1 Exercise A   24
10.1 Exercise B   24
10.2 Exercise A   25
10.2 Exercise B   25
10.3 Exercise A   25
10.3 Exercise B   25
10.4 Exercise A   26
10.4 Exercise B   26
10.5 Exercise A   26
10.5 Exercise B   26
10.6 Exercise A   26
10.6 Exercise B   27

Contents

11 Two-dimensional shapes — 27
11.1 Exercise A — 27
11.1 Exercise B — 27
11.2 Exercise A — 28
11.2 Exercise B — 28
11.3 Exercise A — 29
11.3 Exercise B — 29
11.4 Exercise A — 30
11.4 Exercise B — 31
11.5 Exercise A — 31
11.5 Exercise B — 32

12 Using a formula — 32
12.1 Exercise A — 32
12.1 Exercise B — 33
12.2 Exercise A — 33
12.2 Exercise B — 34

13 Averages — 34
13.1 Exercise A — 34
13.1 Exercise B — 34
13.2 Exercise A — 35
13.2 Exercise B — 35
13.3 Exercise A — 35
13.3 Exercise B — 35
13.4 Exercise A — 36
13.4 Exercise B — 36

14 Solid shapes — 37
14.1 Exercise A — 37
14.1 Exercise B — 37
14.2 Exercise A — 37
14.2 Exercise B — 38

15 Sequences — 38
15.1 Exercise A — 38
15.1 Exercise B — 39
15.2 Exercise A — 39
15.2 Exercise B — 40

16 Probability — 41
16.1 Exercise A — 41
16.1 Exercise B — 41
16.2 Exercise A — 41
16.2 Exercise B — 42
16.3 Exercise A — 42
16.3 Exercise B — 42
16.4 Exercise A — 43
16.4 Exercise B — 43
16.5 Exercise A — 44
16.5 Exercise B — 44

17 Calculating with fractions and decimals — 44
17.1 Exercise A — 44
17.1 Exercise B — 45
17.2 Exercise A — 45
17.2 Exercise B — 45
17.3 Exercise A — 45
17.3 Exercise B — 46

18 Straight line graphs — 46
18.1 Exercise A — 46
18.1 Exercise B — 46
18.2 Exercise A — 47
18.2 Exercise B — 48

19 Transformations — 48
19.1 Exercise A — 48
19.1 Exercise B — 49
19.2 Exercise A — 50
19.2 Exercise B — 50
19.3 Exercise A — 51
19.3 Exercise B — 51
19.4 Exercise A — 52
19.4 Exercise B — 53

20 Real-life graphs — 53
20.1 Exercise A — 53
20.1 Exercise B — 54
20.2 Exercise A — 54
20.2 Exercise B — 54
20.3 Exercise A — 55
20.3 Exercise B — 55

21 Charts, graphs and diagrams — 56
21.1 Exercise A — 56
21.1 Exercise B — 56
21.2 Exercise A — 57
21.2 Exercise B — 57
21.3 Exercise A — 58
21.3 Exercise B — 58
21.4 Exercise A — 59
21.4 Exercise B — 59

22 Mental and written methods — 59
22.1 Exercise A — 59
22.1 Exercise B — 60
22.2 Exercise A — 60
22.2 Exercise B — 60
22.3 Exercise A — 60
22.3 Exercise B — 61
22.4 Exercise A — 61
22.4 Exercise B — 61

23 Bearings and scales   61
23.1 Exercise A   61
23.1 Exercise B   62
23.2 Exercise A   62
23.2 Exercise B   63

24 Using and comparing data   63
24.1 Exercise A   63
24.1 Exercise B   64
24.2 Exercise A   64
24.2 Exercise B   65
24.3 Exercise A   65
24.3 Exercise B   66

25 Percentages   66
25.1 Exercise A   66
25.1 Exercise B   66
25.2 Exercise A   67
25.2 Exercise B   67
25.3 Exercise A   68
25.3 Exercise B   68
25.4 Exercise A   68
25.4 Exercise B   69

26 More algebra skills   69
26.1 Exercise A   69
26.1 Exercise B   70
26.2 Exercise A   70
26.2 Exercise B   70
26.3 Exercise A   71
26.3 Exercise B   71

27 Angles, triangles and polygons   71
27.1 Exercise A   71
27.1 Exercise B   72
27.2 Exercise A   72
27.2 Exercise B   73
27.3 Exercise A   73
27.3 Exercise B   73
27.4 Exercise A   73
27.4 Exercise B   74
27.5 Exercise A   74
27.5 Exercise B   75

28 Ratio and proportion   75
28.1 Exercise A   75
28.1 Exercise B   75
28.2 Exercise A   76
28.2 Exercise B   76

29 Using formulae   76
29.1 Exercise A   76
29.1 Exercise B   77
29.2 Exercise A   77
29.2 Exercise B   78
29.3 Exercise A   78
29.3 Exercise B   78

30 Experimental probability   79
30.1 Exercise A   79
30.1 Exercise B   79
30.2 Exercise A   81
30.2 Exercise B   81

31 Perimeter and area   82
31.1 Exercise A   82
31.1 Exercise B   83
31.2 Exercise A   83
31.2 Exercise B   84
31.3 Exercise A   84
31.3 Exercise B   85
31.4 Exercise A   86
31.4 Exercise B   86

32 Equalities and inequalities   87
32.1 Exercise A   87
32.1 Exercise B   87
32.2 Exercise A   88
32.2 Exercise B   89
32.3 Exercise A   89
32.3 Exercise B   90

33 Accuracy and speed   90
33.1 Exercise A   90
33.1 Exercise B   91
33.2 Exercise A   91
33.2 Exercise B   92

34 Collecting data   92
34.1 Exercise A   92
34.1 Exercise B   93
34.2 Exercise A   94
34.2 Exercise B   94
34.3 Exercise A   95
34.3 Exercise B   95

35 Three-dimensional shapes   96
35.1 Exercise A   96
35.1 Exercise B   96
35.2 Exercise A   97
35.2 Exercise B   97
35.3 Exercise A   98
35.3 Exercise B   98

Contents

36 Sequences   **99**
36.1 Exercise A   99
36.1 Exercise B   99
36.2 Exercise A   99
36.2 Exercise B   100

37 Common factors and common multiples   **100**
37.1 Exercise A   100
37.1 Exercise B   101
37.2 Exercise A   101
37.2 Exercise B   101
37.3 Exercise A   101
37.3 Exercise B   102

38 Averages for large data sets   **102**
38.1 Exercise A   102
38.1 Exercise B   103

38.2 Exercise A   103
38.2 Exercise B   104
38.3 Exercise A   105
38.3 Exercise B   105
38.4 Exercise A   105
38.4 Exercise B   106

39 Graphs   **106**
39.1 Exercise A   106
39.1 Exercise B   107
39.2 Exercise A   107
39.2 Exercise B   108

40 Coordinates and loci   **109**
40.1 Exercise A   109
40.1 Exercise B   109
40.2 Exercise A   109
40.2 Exercise B   109

Homework

Chapter 1

1.1 Exercise A

1

Millions	Hundred thousands	Ten thousands	Thousands	Hundreds	Tens	Units	.	tenths	hundredths	thousandths

Draw a table with the above headings and 4 extra rows.
Write the following numbers in the correct columns.
- **a** 208
- **b** 10 047
- **c** 306.7
- **d** 1054.045

2 Write the following numbers in words.
- **a** 245
- **b** 3076
- **c** 17 881
- **d** 2 360 109

3 Write the following numbers in figures.
- **a** three hundred and seven
- **b** one thousand three hundred and ninety eight
- **c** four thousand and thirty two
- **d** three million three hundred and forty one thousand nine hundred and seven

4 Work out the value of each of the following. Write each answer in **i** figures **ii** words.
- **a** $97 + 234$
- **b** 176×232
- **c** $171\ 288 \div 36$
- **d** 1001×2002

1.1 Exercise B

Work out each of the following.
Write down the value of the digit 6 in the answer.

1 365×10

2 2306×100

3 3642×100

4 $638 \div 10$

5 $7826 \div 10$

6 $34\ 764 \div 100$

7 47.65×10

8 $793.26 \div 10$

Work out each of the following.
Write down the value of the digit 6 in the answer.

9 $0.6148 \times 1\ 000\ 000$

10 $6\ 215\ 104 \div 100\ 000$

11 $0.004\ 643 \times 10\ 000$

12 $286\ 147 \div 10\ 000\ 000$

13 $49.346\ 89 \times 1\ 000\ 000$

14 $6\ 098\ 453 \div 100\ 000$

1.2 Exercise A

1 Copy the number lines and label the numbers shown on the number lines by the arrows.

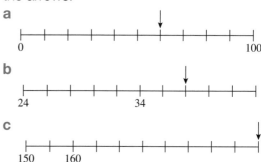

2 Put each list of numbers in order of size starting with the smallest.
- **a** 6 12 9 5 14 19
- **b** 23 8 12 20 17 33
- **c** 114 98 104 76 119 123 105 87

3 From each list of numbers write down the biggest and the smallest number.
- **a** 1035 5013 3051 3015 5031 1053
- **b** Eight million Eighty thousand Eighty Eight thousand
- **c** 40 206 60 204 40 602 20 406 20 604 60 402

4 Draw number lines and use them to find the answers to each of the following. Show clearly how you worked out your answers.

    a The number that is 32 more than 28

    b The number that is 19 less than 100

    c The number that is exactly halfway between 30 and 80

5 Work out each of the following using a number line labelled from 0 to 100 in steps of 10

Check your answers using a calculator

    a 34 + 49   **b** 18 + 65

    c 76 − 38   **d** 98 − 19

    e 16 × 6   **f** 8 × 13

1.2 Exercise B

1 Work out the number that is exactly halfway between each of the following pairs of numbers.

    a 20 and 40   **b** 120 and 130

    c 33 and 41   **d** 32 and 56

2 Find the missing numbers for each of the following:

    a 34 is exactly halfway between 28 and …

    b 40 is exactly halfway between … and 54

    c 39 is exactly halfway between 23 and …

    d 67 is exactly halfway between … and 91

3 Work out the number that is exactly halfway between each of the following pairs of numbers.

    a 78 and 110   **b** 128 and 190

    c 6 and 154   **d** 33 and 81

4 Find the missing number for each of the following:

    a 124 is exactly halfway between 66 and …

    b 165 is exactly halfway between … and 234

1.3 Exercise A

1 Work out

    a 34 + 42   **b** 81 + 39

    c 98 + 54   **d** 76 + 98 + 98

2 Work out

    a 100 − 56   **b** 100 − 72

    c 70 − 36   **d** 140 − 67

3 Work out

    a 87 − 24   **b** 106 − 43

    c 165 − 83   **d** 433 − 302

4 Work out

    a 7 × 8

    b 8 × 8

    c 6 × 12

    d 5 × 9

5 Work out

    a 63 ÷ 7

    b 54 ÷ 9

    c 48 ÷ 6

    d 56 ÷ 7

6 Work out

    a £1.99 × 4

    b 5 × £3.99

    c £5.65 + £2.99

    d £5.08 − 99p

    e £1.49 × 6

    f £10 − 89p

7 From the list of numbers

    3   7   11   23   34   58

    write down

    a two numbers which have a sum of 81

    b two numbers with a difference of 12

    c two numbers greater than 22 and less than 45

8 Use your calculator to work out

    a £43.70 + £34.50

    b £3.56 + £4.91 + £5.67

    c £34.78 + 67p + £20.95

    d £45.84 − £23.71

    e £67 − £32.40

    f £88 − 88p

1.3 Exercise B

1 Complete the following bills

a

	£	Pence
3 pies @ 70p		
4 scones @ 40p		
2 loaves @ 65p		
Total		

b

	£	Pence
2 pizzas @ £3		
3 garlic bread @ £1.50		
3 fries @ £1.20		
Total		

2 An ironing service charges £6.50 per bag of ironing plus a fixed charge of £10
 a How much is charged to iron four bags of clothes?
 b The charge is £49, how many bags of clothes have been ironed?

3 A phone company charges £9.50 per month and then 2p per minute for calls.
 a What is the total cost of making 200 minutes of calls in one month?
 b The total charges for a month are £19.50. How many minutes of calls were made?

4 A man buys four pairs of socks costing £1.50 per pair.
 a How much change does he receive from a £20 note?
 b His change is given using the smallest possible number of notes and coins. How is the change given?

5 The cash price of a DVD player is £250 The credit price is £60 deposit and then 12 monthly payments of £20 How much cheaper is it to pay using cash rather than credit?

6 Niles works for 6 hours earning £8.40 per hour.
 How much does he earn?

7 Archie spends £2.60 on 5 bananas and 4 pears. Pears are 35p each. How much does one banana cost?

8 Joanna goes shopping. This is her shopping bill.

Item	Price (£)
Milk	0.65
Bread	1.06
Bacon	1.99
Total	

 a Work out Joanna's total bill.
 b What change should she get from a £10 note?

9 A bottle of cola in a shop costs 89p. The same bottle in a restaurant costs £2.50 How much more would five bottles of cola cost in the restaurant compared to the shop?

1.4 Exercise A

1 For each pair, which number is bigger? You may use a number line to help you.
 a −4 or +2   **b** −2 or 0
 c +6 or −4   **d** −4 or −6

2 Work out the difference between the pairs of numbers in question **1**

3 For each pair of numbers in question **1**
 i mark the numbers on a number line
 ii work out the number that is exactly halfway between them.

4 Put each set of numbers in order of size, starting with the smallest.
 a 3   −7   1   −2   0
 b −6   4   −4   5   1
 c −9   0   −8   3   −4   −6

5 Work out
 a 45 − 76   **b** −25 + 41
 c −42 − 5 + 12 + 20
 d −34 − 98   **e** −678 + 234
 f −705 − 395

1.4 Exercise B

1 The tables show the temperature in different towns and cities on one day.
For each table **a** and **b**
  i Which place is the warmest?
  ii Which place is the coldest?
  iii Write the names of the places in order starting with the coldest.
  iv Later that day the temperature in each place is 5 degrees colder.
  Write down the new temperatures.

a

Town/City	Temperature (°C)
Paris	0
Vienna	−4
Moscow	−18
Ankara	+23
Rome	+12

b

Town/City	Temperature (°C)
Dallas	+32
Vancouver	−11
Dacca	+27
Tehran	+18
Helsinki	−6

2 Various items were recovered from the beach or the bottom of the sea after a shipwreck of a pirate ship.
The table shows the height / depth at which various items were found.

Item	Height / Depth
Bottle of rum	50 metres below sea level
Barrel	10 metres above sea level
Gold coins	35 metres below sea level
Clothes	4 metres above sea level
Cannonball	60 metres below sea level

a Which items were found on the beach?

b Which item was found at the bottom of the sea?

c What is the difference in height between

  i the barrel and the gold coins

  ii the cannonball and the clothes

  iii the cannonball and the gold coins?

1.5 Exercise A

1 This Eurostar timetable shows train times from Lightown (Waterloo) between 0800 and 1200

LIGHTOWN	Ashton	Cogville	BEETON	DEMSHIRE	Greenville
08.12	–	–	–	11.47	
08.39	09.30	11.29	12.10		
09.09	09.59	–	–	12.53	
09.39	10.31	–	–	–	13.29
09.42	10.40	–	–	–	–
10.12	–	–	–	13.53	
10.39	–	–	–	14.17	
10.42	–	13.24	14.05		
11.39	–	14.21	–	15.23	

a How many trains stop at Beeton?

b How many trains travel directly from Lightown to Demshire without stopping?

c What time does the 1042 Lightown train arrive in Cogville?

d How long does the 0939 train take to get to Greenville?

e Tacey needed to get from Lightown to Demshire by 2 pm.
What is the latest train she could catch to do this?

2 Here is a fare table for a bus route.

Bus station				
£1.00	Town centre			
£1.55	80p	Hospital		
£1.80	£1.35	£1.10	School	
£2.15	£1.60	£1.30	£1.05	Railway station

a How much is the fare from
  i the bus station to the hospital
  ii the school to the railway station
  iii the railway station to the bus station?

b Ada and Les travel from the town centre to the railway station. What is their change from a £10 note?

1.5 Exercise B

1 Look again at this fare table.

Bus station				
£1.00	Town centre			
£1.55	80p	Hospital		
£1.80	£1.35	£1.10	School	
£2.15	£1.60	£1.30	£1.05p	Railway station

The number of tickets sold on one particular journey of this bus is as follows.

Bus station				
9	Town centre			
11	7	Hospital		
6	13	1	School	
12	8	3	2	Railway Station

a Which was the most popular journey?
b How many passengers travelled from the bus station to the hospital?
c How many people were on the bus just after it left the school?

2 The table shows Mr Brown's timetable for one day at school

08:00	Arrive in school
08:20	Staff meeting
08:30	Registration
08:45–09:45	Y8 Mathematics
09:50–10:50	Y13 Statistics
10:50–11:10	Break Duty
11.10–12.10	Y7 Mathematics
12:10–13:10	Lunch
13:10–13.15	Registration
13:15–14.15	Y11 Mathematics
14:20–15:20	Y12 Mathematics

a How long is lunchtime?
b How long is it from the start of Y8 Mathematics to the start of lunchtime?
c How long is spent in registration each day?

d How many hours and minutes is spent in registration during the course of a seven week term?

3 The table shows the distances in miles between some towns and cities.

Allenby			
56	Broxton		
207	188	Carnley	
165	32	100	Dartby

a Which places are furthest apart?
b How far is it from Allenby to Carnley?
c How much further is it from Broxton to Carnley than Allenby to Dartby?

1.6 Exercise A

1 Round the following numbers to the nearest 10
  a 73   **b** 49
  c 113   **d** 675

2 Round the following numbers to the nearest 100
  a 183 **b** 450 **c** 3865 **d** 2026

3 Round these numbers to the nearest 1000
  a 3867   **b** 3078
  c 4500   **d** 23 435

4 Round these numbers to the nearest whole number
  a 4.7 **b** 92.3 **c** 45.5 **d** 902.5

5 Round the following numbers to
  i one decimal place
  ii two decimal places
  iii three decimal places
  a 4.3217 **b** 0.28679 **c** 12.35574
  d 0.0962 **e** 17.4567 **f** 9.5959

6 Round these numbers to one significant figure
  a 36   **b** 52   **c** 318
  d 856   **e** 324.6   **f** 0.647
  g 20.9   **h** 0.065

7 Use a calculator to work out each calculation.
 i Write the full calculator display.
 ii Write the answer to one decimal place.
 iii Write the answer to one significant figure.
 a 7.8×8.9 **b** $23 \div 6.4$
 c 97.31×21.65

1.6 Exercise B

1 a 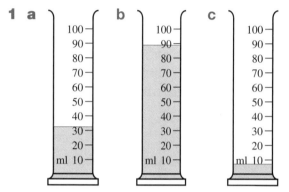 **b** **c**

Look at the measuring cylinders. Estimate the volume of liquid to the nearest 10 ml

2 A piece of string is measured to be 27.6 cm.
 How long is the piece of string
 a to the nearest centimetre?
 b to the nearest 10 cm?

3 13 459 people attended a march in a city centre.
 The organisers claimed 15 000 marched.
 The police claimed 13 000 marched.
 Who is more accurate?
 Explain your answer.

4 Estimate the value of the following.
 In each case write down the numbers used to make the estimates.
 a 9.6×15.1 **b** $20.3 \div 4.1$
 c 98.6×25.2 **d** $61.56 \div 5.89$

5 Use a calculator to work out each calculation.
 i Write down the full calculator display
 ii Write the answer to one decimal place.
 a $15.47 + 32.948$ **b** $\dfrac{21.6 \times 9.79}{2.4}$

c $\dfrac{10.6}{4.8 - 2.88}$ **d** $9.54 \times 45.9 + 18.4$

Chapter 2

2.1 Exercise A

1 State whether each of the following angles is acute, obtuse or reflex.
 a $156°$ **b** $45°$ **c** $232°$ **d** $342°$
 e $78°$ **f** $200°$ **g** $359°$ **h** $5°$

2 For each angle
 a name the angle using letters
 b measure the angle

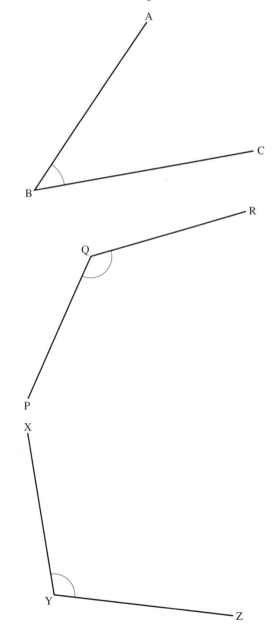

3 Draw these angles accurately
   a 70°   **b** 120°
   c 165°   **d** 55°
   e 118°   **f** 13°

2.1 Exercise B

1 For each of the marked angles
   i State whether the angle is acute, obtuse or reflex
   ii estimate the size of the angle
   iii measure the angle accurately.

a

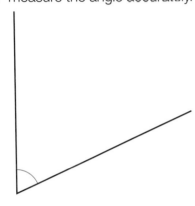

b

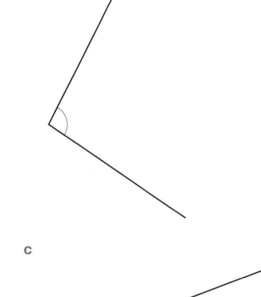

c

d   **e**

2.2 Exercise A

Calculate the missing angles.

1

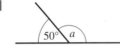

50° *a*

2

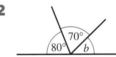

70°
80° *b*

3

c 60°

4

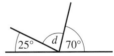

25° *d* 70°

5

130°
e

6

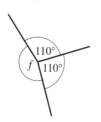

110°
f 110°

7

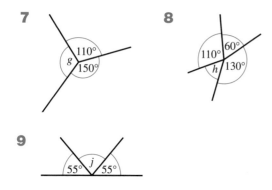

110°
g
150°

8

110° 60°
h 130°

9

55° j 55°

2.2 Exercise B

Calculate the size of the angles marked with letters.

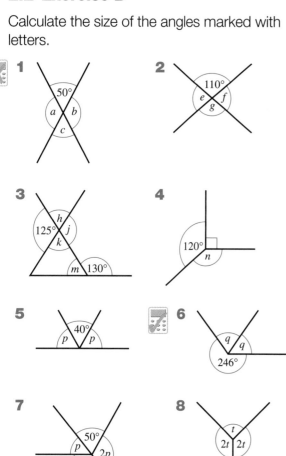

1

50°
a b
c

2

110°
e f
g

3

h
125° j
k
m 130°

4

120°
n

5

40°
p p

6

q q
246°

7

50°
p 2p
2p

8

t
2t 2t

9

74°
w t
v
x 80° 48°

10

a
2a

2.3 Exercise A

For each triangle write down whether it is scalene, isosceles, equilateral or right-angled. Give reasons for your answers.

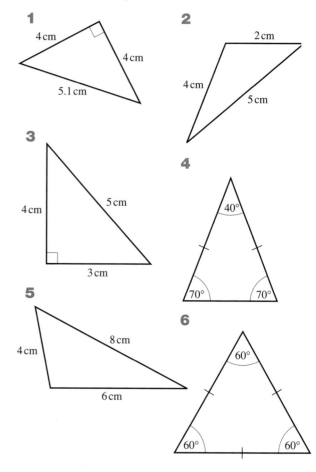

1

4 cm
4 cm
5.1 cm

2

2 cm
4 cm
5 cm

3

4 cm
5 cm
3 cm

4

40°
70° 70°

5

4 cm
8 cm
6 cm

6

60°
60° 60°

2.3 Exercise B

1 Find the size of angle x.

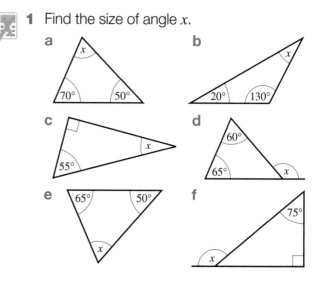

a

x
70° 50°

b

x
20° 130°

c

x
55°

d

60°
65° x

e

65° 50°
x

f

75°
x

2 Find the size of the angles marked with letters.

a

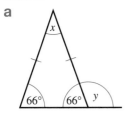

b

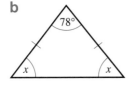

c

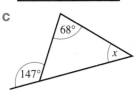

d

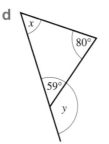

e

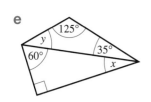

f

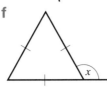

3 Find the angles marked with letters.

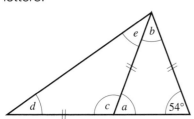

2.4 Exercise A

1 Use a ruler and protractor to draw the following triangles accurately:

   a Triangle *ABC* where *AB* = 8 cm, *AC* = 6 cm and angle *A* = 50°

   b Triangle *DEF* where *DE* = 7 cm, *EF* = 4 cm and angle *E* = 20°

   c Triangle *LMN* where *LM* = 10 cm, *LN* = 9 cm and angle *L* = 125°

   d Triangle *PQR* where *PQ* = 8 cm, angle *Q* = 70° and angle *R* = 65°

   e Triangle *STU* where *TU* = 4 cm, angle *T* = 100° and angle *U* = 35°

2 Make accurate drawings of the following triangles.

a

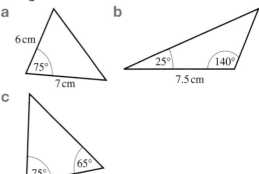

b

c

2.4 Exercise B

1 Using a ruler and compasses, construct the following triangles:

   a Triangle *ABC* where *AB* = 9 cm, *AC* = 6 cm and *BC* = 7 cm

   b Triangle *DEF* where *DE* = 7 cm, *EF* = 5 cm and *DF* = 10 cm

   c Triangle *LMN* where *LM* = 10 cm, *LN* = 9 cm and *MN* = 9 cm

   d Triangle *PQR* where *PQ* = *QR* = *PR* = 7 cm

2 An isosceles triangle has two equal sides of 6 cm and two equal angles of 55°.

   a Draw a sketch of this triangle.

   b Using a ruler and protractor make an accurate drawing of the triangle.

   c Measure and write down the length of the third side.

   d Measure the size of the third angle. How can you tell if your measurement is accurate?

3 Using ruler and compasses, make an accurate drawing of the following shape.

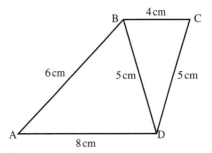

(Hint – construct triangle *ABD* first)

Chapter 3

3.1 Exercise A

1 Write down the square of
- **a** 6
- **b** 4
- **c** 7
- **d** 9
- **e** 10

2 Which of the following numbers are square numbers?
25 32 48 56 64 66 71 81 99

3 Use a calculator to work out
- **a** 17^2
- **b** 24^2
- **c** 54^2
- **d** 49^2
- **e** 19^2
- **f** 2.7^2
- **g** 0.6^2
- **h** 11.9^2
- **i** 20.7^2
- **j** 8.08^2

4 Work out the answers to each part. Write down what you notice.
- **a** 11^2
- **b** 110^2
- **c** 1.1^2
- **d** 0.11^2
- **e** 1100^2

3.1 Exercise B

1 Write down two square numbers with a sum of
- **a** 125
- **b** 37
- **c** 41
- **d** 90
- **e** 50

2 Write down two square numbers with a difference of
- **a** 8
- **b** 9
- **c** 72
- **d** 24
- **e** 36

3 Write down two square numbers which multiply together to give another square number.

4 **a** Work out $7^2 - 6^2$
- **b** Work out $7 + 6$
- **c** Comment on your answers to parts **a** and **b**.

5 **a** Check that $3^2 + 4^2 = 5^2$
- **b** Check that $6^2 + 8^2 = 10^2$
- **c** Predict $9^2 + 12^2$. Check your answer.

3.2 Exercise A

1 Copy and complete
- **a** $\sqrt{16} = 4$ because
.... × .... = 16

- **b** $\sqrt{36} = ...$ because
...... × .... = ...

- **c** $\sqrt{....} = 8$ because
.... × ....= ....

2 Work out
- **a** $\sqrt{9}$
- **b** $\sqrt{81}$
- **c** $\sqrt{49}$
- **d** $\sqrt{1}$
- **e** $\sqrt{100}$

3 For each of the following
- **i** write out the full calculator display
- **ii** write the answer to one decimal place.
- **a** $\sqrt{55}$
- **b** $\sqrt{84}$
- **c** $\sqrt{22}$
- **d** $\sqrt{99}$
- **e** $\sqrt{500}$

4 Put each set of numbers in order starting with the smallest.
- **a** 8.5 $\sqrt{70}$ 2.8^2
- **b** 4.5 $\sqrt{20}$ 2.2^2

5 Put these numbers in order starting with the smallest.
9.1 3.1^2 $\sqrt{82}$ $27 \div 3.1$ 1.01×9

3.2 Exercise B

1 Which is the greater? Show your working.
- **a** $\sqrt{30}$ or 5
- **b** $\sqrt{50}$ or 7
- **c** $\sqrt{70}$ or 8

2 Work out
- **a** **i** $\sqrt{49}$ **ii** $\sqrt{4900}$ **iii** $\sqrt{490\,000}$
- **b** **i** $\sqrt{64}$ **ii** $\sqrt{6400}$ **iii** $\sqrt{640\,000}$

3 Use your calculator to work out
- **a** $\sqrt{23.81}$
- **b** $\sqrt{8.4} + \sqrt{12.7}$
- **c** $\sqrt{23.67} - \sqrt{19.03}$
- **d** $\dfrac{\sqrt{54.76}}{\sqrt{45.67}}$
- **e** $\sqrt{\dfrac{70.31}{34.88}} - \sqrt{\dfrac{30.87}{27.44}}$

3.3 Exercise A

1 Work out the value of
- **a** 2^4
- **b** 4^3
- **c** 5^2
- **d** 5^3
- **e** 10^3

2 Put these numbers in order starting with the smallest
2^3 6^2 2^5 7^2 3^3

3 a Here is a pattern of powers of 2.
Copy and complete the pattern.
$2 \quad 2^2 \quad 2^3 \quad 2^4 \quad 2^5 \quad 2^6 \quad 2^7 \quad 2^8$
$2 \quad 4 \quad 8 \quad ... \quad ... \quad ... \quad ... \quad ...$

b Here is a pattern of powers of 4.
Copy and complete the pattern.
$4 \quad 4^2 \quad 4^3 \quad 4^4$
$4 \quad 16 \quad ... \quad ...$

c What do you notice about your answers to parts **a** and **b**?

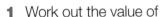

4 Use the power button on the calculator to work out
a 7^3 **b** 9^4 **c** 4^7
d 11^5 **e** 15^3

5 Which number is the larger in each of these pairs of numbers?
a 9^3 or 3^9
b 5^7 or 7^5
c 16^3 or 13^6

3.3 Exercise B

1 Work out the value of
a $2^4 \times 4$ **b** $3^3 \times 5$ **c** $5^3 \times 2^2$

2 Work out
a the difference between 4^3 and 2^5
b the sum of 7^2 and 3^4
c the value of 34^1
d which of these numbers is closest to $100 - 5^3$, 8^2 or 2^7

3 Which of these numbers are cube numbers?
8   9   24   27   36   60   64   100

4 Which number less than 100 is both a square number and a cube number?

5 Put these numbers in order, largest first.
$10^4 \quad 7^7 \quad 9^5 \quad 8^6$

6 Use your calculator to work out
a $6^3 + 7^3 + 8^3$
b $9^5 \div 3^7$
c $3^{10} \times 10^3$

7 Find the largest cube number below 1 000 000

Chapter 4

4.1 Exercise A

1 Every day for a month Lydia counted the number of people waiting at the bus stop as she walked past.
The figures were

6 4 4 5 3 1 3 5 5 0
4 5 3 2 2 4 6 5 3 6
6 3 5 3 4 4 4 3 2 5

Copy and complete the tally chart for her results.

Number of people	Tally	Frequency
0		
1		
2		
3		
4		
5		
6		

2 Natalie records the weather every day at her house. Her choices are Sunny (S), Cloudy but dry (C), Raining (R) or Snowing (Sn).
This is the weather record for January 2006

R   C   C   S   S   S   Sn
Sn   C   R   C   S   S   S
S   C   C   S   S   C   R
R   R   C   S   S   C   C
S   R   R

Copy and complete the tally chart for her results.

Weather	Tally	Frequency
S		
C		
R		
Sn		

4.1 Exercise B

1 Design an observation sheet to collect data about the number of days per week people eat chips.
Invent the first 30 entries.

2 Bud spends time on his mobile phone every day.
The time in minutes he spent on his mobile phone for the last 24 days is as follows.

45	32	16	15	8	42	33
20	14	12	23	6	12	40
12	30	22	9	16	27	34
30	21	5				

a Design and complete a tally chart for this data. Use class intervals 0–9, 10–19, 20–29, 30–39 and 40–49
b Which class interval is the most common?

3 Design a data collection sheet to record people's opinions of a new television programme.

4.2 Exercise A

1 The table shows the number of cups of tea four different staff have during a school day.

Name	Number of cups of tea
Mr Bullips	4
Mr Youngdale	3
Mrs Oliver	7
Mr Lowersat	2

Draw a pictogram to represent this data.
Use a 🥛 to represent two cups of tea.

2 The number of cars owned by each family in a street is as follows.

2 1 3 2 2 1 2 2 1 1 2 2
1 1 2 0 2 3 1 2 2 1 1 1

a Draw a pictogram for this data. Remember to use a key.
b What is the most common number of cars owned?

4.2 Exercise B

1 Jordi finds out how many questions the students in his Maths class got wrong in a test.
The results are

4	3	2	4	4	2	1
4	5	2	0	1	3	3
2	1	3	4	3	5	0
2	1	2	3	2	1	

a Draw a pictogram for this data.
b Altogether how many questions did the students get wrong?
c How many students got all the questions right in the test?

2 The table shows the favourite day of the week of 250 students.

Day	Number choosing it as favourite
Monday	10
Tuesday	25
Wednesday	30
Thursday	20
Friday	65
Saturday	70
Sunday	30

a Draw a pictogram for this data.
Use 👤 to represent a sensible number of students.
b Dave said 'Over half of the students' favourite day is Friday or Saturday'
Is Dave correct? Give a reason for your answer.

4.3 Exercise A

1 Draw a bar chart to show the following data.

Name	Number of pets owned
John	3
Suki	2
Lakhvir	7
Monty	5

2 The bar chart shows the channel being watched by a sample of adults at 10 pm one night.

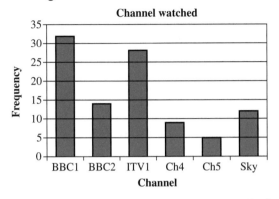

Channel watched

a Which channel was the most popular?

b How many more adults were watching ITV1 compared to Channel 4?

c How many adults were in the sample?

4.3 Exercise B

1 The table shows the temperatures at midday and midnight in five British cities one July night.

City	Midday temperature	Midnight temperature
London	21	15
Cardiff	23	16
Birmingham	24	13
Glasgow	17	9
Manchester	19	11

Draw a dual bar chart to show this data.

2 The dual bar chart shows the number of male and female pupils from each year group late for school one Monday morning.

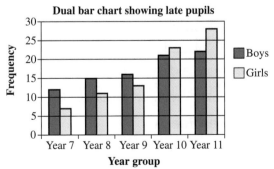

Dual bar chart showing late pupils

a Which year group had the most pupils late?

b Comment on two differences between the lateness of boys and girls at the school.

c How many pupils were late to school that Monday?

d The table shows the results for lateness the next day.

Year	Boys late	Girls late
7	9	4
8	10	8
9	12	13
10	16	17
11	18	23

i Draw a component bar chart for this data.

ii Give one advantage of showing the Tuesday data in a component bar chart rather than a dual bar chart.

iii Give one advantage of showing the Monday data in a dual bar chart rather than a component bar chart.

e On Wednesday one year group was given a special assembly about the importance of being in school on time. Which year group do you think it was? Give a reason for your answer.

Chapter 5

5.1 Exercise A

1 Copy and complete the multiplication tables

a

×	3	−5	−8
4		−20	
7			
−9			72

b

×	4	6	−7
−2	−8		
−5			35
9			

2 Work out

a $32 \div -4$ b $-24 \div -8$

c $35 \div -7$ d $60 \div -10$

e $-63 \div -9$ f $-88 \div 8$

g $-54 \div 6$ h $63 \div -7$

3 Use your calculator to find

a 15×-8 b $-351 \div -9$

c -34×-9 d $-680 \div 17$

5.1 Exercise B

1 Work out

a $2 \times -3 \times 4$ b $-8 \times -1 \times 4$

c $(-4)^3$ d $(-8)^2$

e 40×-50 f -100×-200

g $-80 \div 20$ h $-440 \div -44$

2 List the answers to these sums in order, starting with the smallest

-9×3 $20 \div -4$ 5×6

-7×-5 $50 \div -25$

3 You are given that $135 \times 28 = 3780$
Write down the value of each of the following and then check your answers using a calculator.

a -135×-28 b $3780 \div -135$

c $-3780 \div 28$ d -135×28

5.2 Exercise A

1 Copy and complete the table for this number machine.

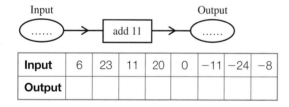

Input	6	23	11	20	0	−11	−24	−8
Output								

2 Copy and complete the table for this number machine.

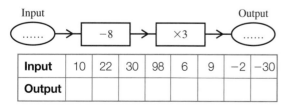

Input	10	22	30	98	6	9	−2	−30
Output								

3 Copy and complete the table for this number machine.

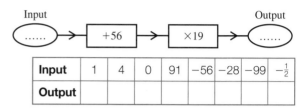

Input	1	4	0	91	−56	−28	−99	$-\frac{1}{2}$
Output								

5.2 Exercise B

1 Copy and complete the table for this number machine.

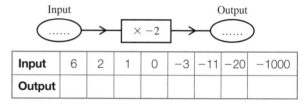

Input	6	2	1	0	−3	−11	−20	−1000
Output								

2 Copy and complete the table for this number machine.

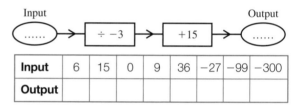

Input	6	15	0	9	36	−27	−99	−300
Output								

3 Copy and complete the table for this number machine.

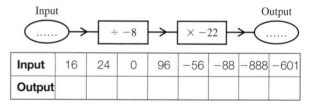

Input	16	24	0	96	−56	−88	−888	−601
Output								

4 a Copy and complete the instruction boxes to make the number machine work.

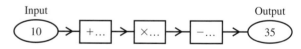

b Find a different set of instruction boxes that work in part **a**.

5.3 Exercise A

1 Here is a number machine

a Work out the output when the input is 12
b Draw the inverse number machine.
c Work out the input when the output is 18

2 Here is a number machine.

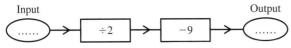

a Work out the output when the input is 20
b Draw the inverse number machine.
c Work out the input when the output is 7

3 Here is a number machine

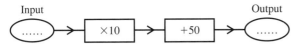

a Work out the output when the input is 30
b Draw the inverse number machine.
c Work out the input when the output is 110

 4 Copy and complete the table for this number machine.

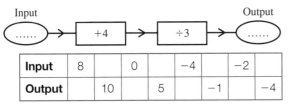

Input	8		0		−4		−2	
Output		10		5		−1		−4

5 Here is a number machine

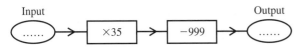

a Work out the output when the input is 76
b Draw the inverse number machine.
c Work out the input when the output is −894

5.3 Exercise B

 1 Here is a number machine

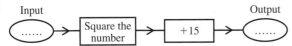

a Work out the output when the input is 4
b Draw the inverse number machine.
c Work out the input when the output is 64

2 Here is a number machine

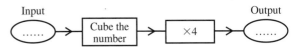

a Work out the output when the input is 2
b Draw the inverse number machine.
c Work out the input when the output is 4000

3 Jane thinks of a number. She multiplies it by 5 and then adds 8. Her answer is 43
a Draw a number machine for this calculation.
b Draw the inverse number machine.
c Find the number Jane was thinking of.

 4 Quinn thinks of a number. He cube roots it, then squares it to get an answer of 81 What number was he thinking of?

5.4 Exercise A

 1 Work out the following. Show each step of your working.
a $2 + 3 \times 4$ b $7 + 3 \times 2$
c $10 - 6 \div 3$ d $9 \div 9 + 10$
e $2 \times 3 + 4 \times 5$ f $(8 - 2) + 2 \times 3$
g $28 \div (14 \div 2)$ h $\frac{1}{2}$ of $(9^2 - 5)$

 2 Use a scientific calculator to work out the following.
a $13 + 45 \times 22$
b $980 - 321 \div 3$
c $47 + 48 \times 49$
d $12 + 13 \times 14 + 15$
e $(76 + 21 - 15) \div (43 - 23)$
f $67^2 - 32^3 \times 35$
g $8^3 - (11 + 5 \times 4)$
h $\frac{1}{5}$ of $(5 + 10 \times 15 + 20)^2$

5.4 Exercise B

1 Copy each calculation and insert **one** pair of brackets to make it correct.

   a $3 + 5 \times 2 + 8 - 4 = 49$

   b $3 + 5 \times 2 + 8 - 4 = 17$

   c $3 + 5 \times 2 + 8 - 4 = 20$

   d $3 + 5 \times 2 + 8 - 4 = 33$

2 Copy each calculation and insert **two** pairs of brackets to make it correct.

   a $2 + 3 \times 4 + 5 - 6 \times 7 = 3$

   b $2 + 3 \times 4 + 5 - 6 \times 7 = 105$

   c $2 + 3 \times 4 + 5 - 6 \times 7 = 13$

   d $2 + 3 \times 4 + 5 - 6 \times 7 = -97$

3 **a** Use the digits 3, 4, 5 and 6 to make the target number of 37
Each digit can be used only once. Any operations can be used.

   b Use the digits 3, 4, 5 and 6 and the same rules to make other target numbers between 30 and 40

4 Use the digits 7, 8 and 9 to make the following target numbers.

   a 6   **b** 10

   c 65   **d** 0.6

   e 7.875

5 Work out

   a $\dfrac{3.8 \times 1.6}{4.8 \div 0.65}$

   b $\dfrac{2.1 + 1.8 \times 0.7}{34 - 26.88}$

   c $\sqrt{\dfrac{5.08 + 2.97}{4.7^3}}$

Chapter 6

6.1 Exercise A

1 Write each of these in simplest form.

   a $x + x$

   b $y + y + y + y$

   c $m + m + m + n + n$

2 Write each of these without the multiplication symbol.

   a $4 \times x$

   b $5 \times p + 10$

   c $2 \times d + 3 \times e + 4 \times f$

3 Look at this number machine

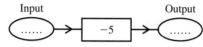

   a What is the output when the input is 12?

   b What is the input when the output is 4?

   c Complete the word formula:

      Output = ………… − ……

   d Use the letter x for the input and y for the output to complete this formula

      …… = ……− ……..

4 Repeat question **3** for this number machine.

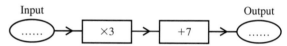

6.1 Exercise B

1 Rewrite these formulae using letter symbols of your choice. Remember to state what the letters stand for.

   a Area of a rectangle equals length of rectangle multiplied by width of rectangle.

   b Perimeter of a square equals four times the length of one side.

2 In each of the following do the letter symbols have only one value or could they have lots of values? Explain your answer each time.

   a

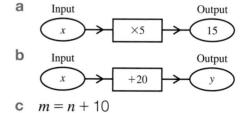

   b

   c $m = n + 10$

3 A box of golf balls contains g golf balls.

   a **i** Tiger buys 3 boxes of golf balls. How many golf balls does he have?

      ii He loses two of them in a river. How many does he have now?

   b Colin buys 5 boxes of golf balls to add to the 14 he already has. How many golf balls does he have altogether now?

   c How many golf balls do Tiger and Colin now have between them?

6.2 Exercise A

1 Copy and complete this table.

	Expression	Meaning in words
a	$x - 5$	subtract 5 from x
b	$y + 4$	
c	$4w$	
d		divide t by 5
e	$\dfrac{p + 9}{5}$	
f		divide m by 4 then subtract 3 from the result

2 Match the expression in the left hand column with the one from the right hand column that means the same.

$3x + 1$	$x + \frac{1}{3}$
$x + 1 \div 3$	$x + 1 + x + 1 + x + 1$
$(x + 1) \div 3$	x^3
$3(x + 1)$	$x \div 3 + 1$
$\dfrac{x}{3} + 1$	$\dfrac{x + 1}{3}$
$x \times x \times x$	$x + x + x + 1$

3 **a** Write a formula for the output, y, for this number machine.

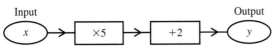

   b Draw a number machine showing the output, y, for the input, x, for this formula: $y = \dfrac{x - 9}{10}$

4 Godfrey earns £10 per week delivering papers and £y per week washing cars.

   a How much does he earn in total in one week?

   b How much does he earn in total in 20 weeks?

6.2 Exercise B

1 Write a formula for the output y for each of these number machines.

   a

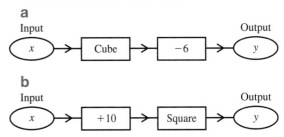

   b

Input   Output

x → $+10$ → Square → y

2 Explain why $a + b + c$ is not a formula.

3 There are s sweets in Tom's bag and t sweets in Betty's bag.

   a Write an expression for the total number of sweets in the two bags.

   b If Betty has twice as many sweets as Tom, write a formula connecting s and t.

4 Dolly has y marbles to share between herself and f friends. How many marbles will each person get?

6.3 Exercise A

1 Simplify

   a $a + a$

   b $b + b + b + b$

   c $c + c + c + d + d$

   d $x + x + x - x - x + y + y - y$

   e $m + m + m + m + n + n + n - m - m - n + p$

2 Simplify each of the following expressions.

   a $4x + 3x$ **b** $7y - 2y$

   c $8p + 3p - 5p$ **d** $v + 4v - 3$

   e $6c + 2d + c - d$ **f** $4f + 2 - 3f + 6$

3 Simplify
  a $2 \times 3 \times x$ **b** $3 \times 4 \times y \times y$
  c $j \times 5 \times 2 \times j$ **d** $3x \times 2$
  e $4x \times 3x^2$ **f** $7a \times 4b$

6.3 Exercise B

1 Simplify each of these expressions
  a $3x - 5x$
  b $y - 4y$
  c $5s - 3 + 2s + 8$
  d $-6u - u$
  e $-2r + p + 5r - 3p$
  f $-a - b - c - a - b - c$

2 Simplify each of the following.
  a $8a \div 4$ **b** $10b \div 5b$ **c** $\dfrac{100c}{25c}$

3 A square has side length of $2x - y$. Find an expression for the perimeter of the square.

4 A rectangle has an area of $24x$ cm². Write down 8 possible pairs of values for the length and width of this rectangle.

5 Copy and complete the addition square and the multiplication square.

+	$2x + 3y$	$5x - y$
$4x$		
		$6x - 2y$

×	$3y$	$5x$
$4x$		
		$60x$

6.4 Exercise A

1 Work out the values of the following expressions when $p = 3$, $q = 4$ and $r = 6$
  a $p + q$ **b** $r - p$
  c qr **d** $7q + r$
  e $2pqr$ **f** $3 + rq$
  g $2q - p$ **h** $\dfrac{r}{2}$
  i $\dfrac{12}{q}$ **j** $\dfrac{q}{4} + \dfrac{18}{r}$

2 Work out the values of the following expressions when $d = 2$, $e = 5$ and $f = 10$
  a $de - f$ **b** $fed - def$
  c $20d + 30e + 40f$ **d** $3e - 5d + 2f$
  e $2e + fd$ **f** $10e(f - 4d)$
  g $3df - 4e$ **h** $de + ef + fd$

6.4 Exercise B

1 Repeat Exercise A question **1** for $p = 3$, $q = -4$ and $r = -6$

2 Repeat Exercise A question **2** for $d = -2$, $e = 5$ and $f = -10$

3 Work out the value of the following expressions when $a = 1$, $b = -3$ and $c = -8$
  a a^2 **b** $2b^2$
  c $3c^2$ **d** $a^2b^2 - (ab)^2$

4 Work out the value of the following expressions on your calculator when $m = 2.8$, $n = -3.6$ and $p = 0.3$
  a mnp **b** $m - p - n$
  c $n^2 - p^2$ **d** $\dfrac{mp - nm}{pn}$

Chapter 7

7.1 Exercise A

1 Work out
  a 19×6 **b** 43×5
  c 317×4 **d** 543×8
  e 42×13 **f** 67×29
  g 237×36 **h** 347×82

2 Work out
  a $63 \div 9$ **b** $42 \div 7$
  c $48 \div 6$ **d** $56 \div 8$

3 The product of two whole numbers is 30 Write down two possible pairs of numbers.

4 **a** Use a calculator to work out 36×79
  b Copy and complete
    i _____ $\div 36 = 79$
    ii _____ $\div 79 = 36$

5 Given that $56 \times 637 = 35\,672$, copy and complete
  a $35\,672 \div 56 =$ _____
  b $35\,672 \div 637 =$ _____

7.1 Exercise B

1 For each part write down the units digit of the answer. You do **not** need to do the whole calculation.
  a 46×72 **b** 56×91
  c 38×75 **d** 793×279

2 Without doing the whole calculation, which of the following are incorrect? Explain your answer.
  a $46 \times 63 = 2897$
  b $39 \times 91 = 3549$
  c $209 \times 67 = 14\,005$

3 Coaches can seat 53 people.
  a How many coaches are needed to seat 924 people?
  b Each person pays 85p for their journey.
    How much do the 924 people pay altogether
    i in pence
    ii in pounds and pence?

4 Each month Geoff saves £45. How many months before he has £1000?

7.2 Exercise A

1 Find the factors of
  a 9   **b** 14   **c** 18   **d** 22   **e** 30

2 Here is a list of numbers.
  2 4 5 6 10 20 50 100
  Which numbers in the list are factors of
  a 50   **b** 60   **c** 100   **d** 200

3 Find the factors of
  a 35   **b** 36   **c** 60
  d 100   **e** 144

4 Find all the factors of 200

7.2 Exercise B

1 Write down a number that is
  a even and a factor of 14
  b odd and a factor of 14
  c a square number and a factor of 32
  d a number that is a factor of 70 and whose digits add up to 8

2 Write down two factors of 30 so that they
  a have a sum of 15
  b have a difference of 12
  c are both even
  d are both odd

3 Use a calculator to find a factor of 900 that is
  a greater than 30 and less than 40
  b a square number
  c a different square number
  d above 300

4 Use a calculator to find a number that is a factor of both
  a 38 and 95
  b 46 and 115
  c 111 and 296

5 Work out the sum of all the factors of 24

6 Find two factors of 812 that have a difference of 1

7.3 Exercise A

1 Write down the first five multiples of
  a 3   **b** 4   **c** 6   **d** 7   **e** 9

2 Here is a list of numbers:
  1 2 3 4 5 10 30 35 45 80
  Which numbers in the list are multiples of
  a 4   **b** 5   **c** 10   **d** 20?

3 Here is a list of numbers:
  6 12 18 24 30 36 42 48
  Which numbers in the list are multiples of
  a 6   **b** 12   **c** 18   **d** 4?

4 Write down the first five multiples of
  a 16   **b** 21   **c** 37   **d** 48

5 Here is a list of numbers:
80 81 82 83 84 85 86
Which number in the list are multiples of
a 12 **b** 14 **c** 17 **d** 21?

7.3 Exercise B

1 Write down a number that is
   a even and a multiple of 5
   b even and a multiple of 11
   c a square number and a multiple of 12

2 Write down
   a two multiples of 7 that have a sum of 21
   b two multiples of 10 that have a sum of 100
   c two multiples of 12 that have a difference of 24
   d two multiples of 50 that have a difference of 250

3 Use a calculator to find a multiple of 18 that is
   a greater than 140 and less than 150
   b greater than 230 and less than 240
   c also a multiple of 15
   d also a multiple of 21

4 Use a calculator to find a number that is a multiple of both
   a 7 and 20 **b** 9 and 15
   c 11 and 31 **d** 47 and 56

5 Donna says that 91 is a multiple of 13
Is she correct? Explain your answer.

7.4 Exercise A

1 Find the three prime numbers in each of these lists
   a 4 5 6 7 8 9 10 11
   b 13 15 17 19 21
   c 20 23 26 29 32 35 38 41

2 Find the three prime numbers in each of these lists
   a 51 53 55 57 59 61 63
   b 70 73 75 79 82 83
   c 89 91 93 95 97 99 101

3 Decide whether each of these numbers is prime.
   a 105 **b** 111 **c** 133 **d** 142
   e 161 **f** 163 **g** 343 **h** 511

4 Use a calculator to show that 1147 has a factor of 31

7.4 Exercise B

1 Write down a prime number that is also
   a a factor of 16
   b a factor of 35
   c a factor of 81

2 Work out the prime factors of
   a 22 **b** 30 **c** 40 **d** 55

3 Archie says that the sum of two prime numbers is always an odd number.
Give an example which shows that Archie is wrong.

4 The sum of the prime numbers 3 and 5 is 8, a cube number.
   a Show that there is not another pair of prime numbers which add to give 8
   b Show that there is not a pair of prime numbers which add to give 27
   c Can you find 2 prime numbers which add to give the next cube number after 27?

5 Work out the prime factors of
   a 54 **b** 69 **c** 75 **d** 120

Chapter 8

8.1 Exercise A

1 Convert each of the following into centimetres.
   a 50 mm **b** 2.5 m
   c 42 mm **d** 31 m

2 Convert each of the following into grams.
   a 4 kg **b** 7.1 kg
   c 0.8 kg **d** 2.6 kg

3 Convert each of the following into litres.
  a 2000 ml   **b** 3500 ml
  c 42 000 ml   **d** 750 ml

4 Copy and complete this table.

mm	cm	m	km
2000			
	3000		
		4000	
			32

5 Copy and complete this table.

g	kg	tonnes
3000		
	200	
		40

6 Write these measures in order of size, smallest first.
  a 482 m, 2148 cm, 0.7 km, 50 000 mm, 82 000 cm
  b 2 tonnes, 307 g, 1.8 kg, 0.04 kg, 3750 kg
  c 3 l, 2847 ml, 2 ml, 0.7 l, 392 ml

8.1 Exercise B

1 Add together 40 cm, 250 mm and 35 cm.

2 Subtract 240 g from 3 kg.
Give your answer in
  a grams   **b** kilograms

3 How many 50 millilitre glasses of cola can you pour from a 2 litre bottle?

4 A shop has 40 kg of grapes.
They sell 30 kg and give away 1500 g.
How many kilograms of grapes does the shop have left?

5 Add together 750 g, 1.5 kg, 0.9 kg and 800 g.

6 A joiner needs 30 lengths of wood each 350 cm long.
Calculate the total length of wood needed. Give your answer in metres.

7 A dress-maker wants to cut pieces of material which are 35 cm long from a 10 m length of fabric.
  a How many 35 cm lengths can be cut from this fabric?
  b How much material will be left over?

8.2 Exercise A

1 Use the conversions 2.5 cm = 1 inch and 12 inches = 1 foot to convert the following to centimetres.
  a 4 inches   **b** 8 inches
  c 3 feet   **d** 10 feet

2 Convert the following to miles
  a 24 km   **b** 60 km
  c 120 km   **d** 144 km

3 Use the conversion 25 g = 1 ounce to convert the following to grams.
  a 3 ounces   **b** 5 ounces
  c 10 ounces   **d** 40 ounces

4 Convert the following to litres
  a 3 gallons   **b** 30 gallons
  c 50 gallons   **d** 200 gallons

5 Use the conversion 2.5 cm = 1 inch to convert the following to inches.
  a 25 cm   **b** 55 cm
  c 95 cm   **d** 124.5 cm

6 Convert the following to pounds
  a 6 kg   **b** 14 kg
  c 17.5 kg   **d** 0.8 kg

8.2 Exercise B

1 Ishmail is exactly 6 feet tall. Estimate his height in centimetres.

2 How many pints of milk are there in a 6 litre carton?

3 The distance from Scunthorpe to Huddersfield is 60 miles. How many kilometres is this?

4 Vincent paints a picture which measures 24 cm by 21 cm. Will it fit into his frame which is 12 inches by 9 inches? Show your working.

5 Baby Niles weighs 5.2 kg. What is Niles's weight in pounds?

6 Quinlan owns a small vineyard. His vines produce 100 pints of wine. How many 750 ml bottles can he fill?

8.3 Exercise A

1 Write down the most suitable metric unit for measuring
  a the time to walk to the front door
  b the weight of an apple
  c the amount of water in a bath
  d the length of a toe-nail.

2 Write down the most suitable imperial unit for measuring
  a the length of a crocodile
  b the time to run a marathon
  c the weight of a hippopotamus
  d the amount of water in a glass.

3 For each of the following lines
  a estimate the length of the line in centimetres
  b measure the length of the line in centimetres
  c find the difference between your estimate and the actual length of the line.
  Line 1
  _____

  Line 2

  Line 3

4 Write down the number indicated by the arrow on each of these scales.
  a

    2   3

  b

    10   20

c
    200

    100

d
    22

    12

8.3 Exercise B

1 Work out the difference between the readings on these two speedometers.

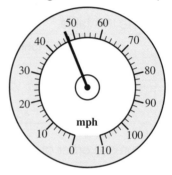

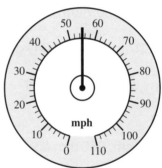

2 The diagram shows a man who is 6 feet tall standing by a house.

Estimate the height of the house in
  a feet   **b** metres

3 The speedometer shows the speed of a car travelling along a road.

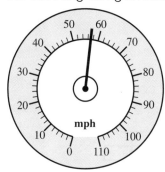

The speed limit on the road is 90 kilometres per hour.
Is the car breaking the speed limit?

4 One kilogram of lamb costs £5.95
What is the cost of
a   400 g of lamb   b   1 pound of lamb?

5 Which is heavier, a 13 ounce mouse or a 315 g jar of jam?
Show your working.

Chapter 9

9.1 Exercise A

1 What numbers must be put in the boxes to make each equation true?

a $\square - 7 = 3$ b $20 \div \square = 4$

c $\square \times 3 - 2 = 10$

d $15 - 10 \div \square = 10$

e $24 \div \square + 3 = 5$

f $\square \div 7 - 6 = 1$

2 Solve these equations by inspection.

a $4x = 8$ b $\dfrac{y}{3} = 24$

c $30 = g + 20$ d $w - 10 = 9$

3 Draw a number machine for each equation. Solve the equation by working backwards.

a $x - 8 = 12$ b $3t - 7 = 20$

c $6f + 9 = 15$ d $\dfrac{m}{3} - 2 = 5$

4 What was my number in each of these 'think of a number' problems?

a   I think of a number, divide by 4 and get 6

b   I think of a number, multiply by 3, then subtract 4 and get 5

c   I think of a number, divide by 5, then add 6 and get 11

9.1 Exercise B

1 Solve the following equations.

a $a + 8 = 3$ b $b + 8 = -6$

c $c - 9 = -6$ d $d + 3 = -10$

e $3e = -12$ f $-4f = -28$

g $\dfrac{g}{3} = -5$ h $\dfrac{-h}{4} = -4$

2 Solve the following equations by working backwards.

a $3z + 12 = 9$ b $-3y - 6 = 9$

c $\dfrac{x}{5} + 3 = 1$ d $\dfrac{-w}{3} - 4 = -5$

e $\dfrac{v}{8} - 4 = -2$ f $4u - 10 = -6$

3 a Solve the equation $3x + 4 = 16$

b Find three more equations with the same solution.

9.2 Exercise A

1 Solve the following equations using the balance method. Show your method clearly.

a $x + 3 = 20$ b $y - 8 = 12$

c $3p = 21$ d $\dfrac{e}{5} = 30$

e $t + 9 = 21$ f $7g = 28$

g $\dfrac{m}{10} = 4$ h $n - 40 = 30$

2 Solve the following equations using the balance method. Show your method clearly.

a $3m + 4 = 19$ b $4p - 1 = 7$

c $\dfrac{q}{3} - 1 = 5$ d $\dfrac{r}{4} + 5 = 12$

e $9y + 2 = 29$ f $8x - 9 = 23$

g $\dfrac{s}{9} + 1 = 10$ h $31 = 1 + \dfrac{t}{2}$

9.2 Exercise B

1 Solve the following equations using the balance method. Show your method clearly.

   a $a + 8 = 3$ **b** $b - 7 = -4$

   c $c + 11 = -1$ **d** $5d = -10$

   e $-4e = -32$ **f** $f - 9 = 3$

   g $\dfrac{g}{4} = -3$ **h** $\dfrac{h}{-3} = -2$

2 Solve the following equations using the balance method. Show your method clearly.

   a $3z + 7 = 1$ **b** $4y - 3 = -11$

   c $\dfrac{x}{3} + 9 = 1$ **d** $\dfrac{w}{4} - 3 = -7$

3 Match the equations to the solutions.

Equations	Solutions
$4x = -8$	$x = -16$
$3x + 5 = -16$	$x = -7$
$x - 9 = -7$	$x = -2$
$\dfrac{x}{2} + 3 = -5$	$x = 2$

2 Copy the diagram for each part.

   a

   i Shade $\frac{2}{3}$

   ii Copy and complete

     $\frac{2}{3} = \ldots\ldots \% = 0.666\ldots$

   b

   i Shade $\frac{1}{4}$

   ii Copy and complete

     $\frac{1}{4} = \ldots\ldots\% = \ldots\ldots$

   c

   i Shade $\frac{2}{5}$

   ii Copy and complete

     $\frac{2}{5} = \ldots\ldots\% = \ldots\ldots\ldots$

3 Make three copies of this shape.

On one copy of the shape shade in

   a $\frac{1}{2}$ **b** $\frac{3}{4}$ **c** $\frac{7}{8}$

Chapter 10

10.1 Exercise A

1 Look at each rectangle and work out

   i the fraction shaded

   ii the fraction unshaded

   iii the percentage shaded

   iv the percentage unshaded.

   a 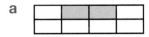   **b**

   c    **d**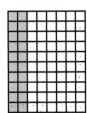

10.1 Exercise B

1 Copy and complete

Fraction	Decimal	Percentage
$\frac{1}{2}$		
	0.2	
		90%
$\frac{3}{4}$		
	0.25	
		33.3…
$\frac{4}{5}$		
	0.666…	
		12.5

2 What fraction of a turn does the minute hand turn through between
- **a** 9.30 pm and 9.45 pm
- **b** 2.50 pm and 3.20 pm
- **c** 12.25 pm and 12.45 pm
- **d** 7.55 am and 8.05 am

3 a Asif said that $\frac{1}{10}$ is the same as the decimal 0.1
Explain why Asif is correct.
- **b** Tony said that $\frac{1}{4}$ was the same as the decimal 0.4
Explain why Tony is wrong.

10.2 Exercise A

1 Work out
- **a** $\frac{1}{2}$ of 20 metres
- **b** $\frac{1}{4}$ of £100
- **c** $\frac{1}{5}$ of £55
- **d** $\frac{1}{8}$ of 16 cm
- **e** one third of 27 miles
- **f** one tenth of 150 kg
- **g** one hundredth of 7000

2 Work out
- **a** $\frac{2}{3}$ of £15
- **b** $\frac{3}{5}$ of 35 yards
- **c** $\frac{7}{10}$ of 200 metres
- **d** $\frac{6}{7}$ of 14

3 Use a calculator to work out
- **a** $\frac{1}{2}$ of £158
- **b** $\frac{1}{4}$ of £856
- **c** $\frac{2}{3}$ of 846 kg
- **d** $\frac{5}{9}$ of 1044

10.2 Exercise B

1 Sweets are sold in different sized bags. In each bag $\frac{1}{3}$ are chocolate, the rest are toffee.
- **a** In a bag of 60 sweets, how many are
   - **i** chocolate
   - **ii** toffee?
- **b** In a bag with 24 chocolates, how many are
   - **i** toffee
   - **ii** in the bag altogether?

2 Put these amounts in order, starting with the smallest.
$\frac{1}{3}$ of 60 $\frac{1}{2}$ of 36 $\frac{3}{4}$ of 32 $\frac{2}{5}$ of 55

3 A shop has 12 000 DVDs available to rent. $\frac{1}{5}$ of the DVDs are for children. How many are **not** for children?

4 Zoltan has 34 371 stamps in his collection. $\frac{4}{9}$ of the stamps are from Hungary. How many of his collection of stamps are from Hungary?

10.3 Exercise A

Copy and complete this table

100%	20	50	64	400
10%				40
5%			3.2	
15%	3			
50%		25		
25%				100
75%	15			
20%		10		
40%			25.6	
60%				240
45%			28.8	
95%	19			
200%		100		
300%				1200

10.3 Exercise B

1 There are 1000 pupils in a school. 20% are Sixth-Formers. How many are Sixth-Formers?

2 Work out
- **a** 24% of 250
- **b** 18% of 30
- **c** 47% of 80
- **d** 17.5% of £300
- **e** 82% of 940 m
- **f** 71.4% of 3000 cm
- **g** 8.5% of 900
- **h** 1.4% of 3200

3 A baby hippo grows by 17% in one month. If it begins the month weighing 80 kg, how much does it weigh at the end of the month?

10.4 Exercise A

1 Sort the following lists of decimals into ascending order.
  a   3.7   3.07   3.27   3.2   3.72
  b   10.6   6.01   1.06   10.06   6.1   1.6
  c   0.56   0.06   0.05   0.65   0.065

2 Sort the following lists of percentages into descending order.
  a   47.51%   74.15%   74.51%   47.15%
  b   24%   23.99%   24.01%   24.1%   23.9%
  c   3.8%   30.8%   3.08%   0.308%   0.38%

3 Convert the following fractions into decimals.
Write the fractions in ascending order.
  a $\frac{1}{2}$ $\frac{3}{4}$ $\frac{1}{5}$ $\frac{3}{8}$
  b $\frac{2}{7}$ $\frac{5}{11}$ $\frac{1}{9}$ $\frac{8}{15}$
  c $\frac{4}{11}$ $\frac{8}{21}$ $\frac{1}{3}$ $\frac{4}{9}$

10.4 Exercise B

1 Write the following in ascending order.
  a $\frac{1}{5}$ 19%   0.21
  b $\frac{3}{10}$ 0.28   29%
  c $\frac{1}{4}$ 24%   0.251
  d $\frac{1}{8}$ 11%   0.12

2 Which is smaller, $\frac{2}{3}$ or 0.67? You must show your working.

3 Write the following in descending order.
  a $\frac{1}{6}$ 16%   0.166
  b $\frac{1}{9}$ 11%   0.12
  c $\frac{7}{19}$ 35%   0.36
  d $\frac{10}{11}$ 91%   0.909

10.5 Exercise A

1 Copy and complete.
  a $\frac{1}{2} = \frac{\square}{4} = \frac{3}{\square}$ **b** $\frac{1}{8} = \frac{2}{\square} = \frac{\square}{24}$
  c $\frac{1}{11} = \frac{\square}{22} = \frac{3}{\square}$ **d** $\frac{1}{20} = \frac{\square}{40} = \frac{3}{\square}$

2 Write each set of fractions with a common denominator.
  a $\frac{1}{2}$ $\frac{1}{4}$ $\frac{1}{5}$ **b** $\frac{1}{3}$ $\frac{1}{5}$ $\frac{1}{6}$ **c** $\frac{1}{4}$ $\frac{1}{7}$ $\frac{1}{10}$

3 Write down three equivalent fractions to each of the following fractions.
  a $\frac{2}{3}$ **b** $\frac{3}{4}$ **c** $\frac{4}{5}$ **d** $\frac{9}{10}$

10.5 Exercise B

1 Put each set of fractions in order from the smallest to the biggest.
  a $\frac{1}{2}$ $\frac{3}{5}$ $\frac{3}{7}$ **b** $\frac{3}{8}$ $\frac{7}{16}$ $\frac{5}{12}$
  c $\frac{1}{7}$ $\frac{3}{14}$ $\frac{5}{21}$ **d** $\frac{9}{10}$ $\frac{19}{20}$ $\frac{37}{40}$

2 Which of these fractions is greater than $\frac{2}{5}$?
   $\frac{1}{4}$ $\frac{3}{7}$ $\frac{5}{8}$ $\frac{3}{10}$

3 Show that $\frac{12}{13}$ is greater than $\frac{11}{12}$

4 Alexander says that $\frac{1}{16}$ is exactly halfway between $\frac{1}{10}$ and $\frac{1}{22}$
Show that Alexander is wrong.

10.6 Exercise A

1 In each part simplify your answer where possible.
  a   Write 4 as a fraction of 9
  b   Write 3 as a fraction of 12
  c   Write 12 as a fraction of 36
  d   Write 5 miles as a fraction of 50 miles.
  e   Write 20 tonnes as a fraction of 40 tonnes.
  f   Write 11 cm³ as a fraction of 77 cm³.

2 In each part simplify your answer as much as possible.
  a   Write 20 cm as a fraction of 1 m.
  b   Write 150 g as a fraction of 1 kg.
  c   Write 25p as a fraction of £1
  d   Write 800 m as a fraction of 1 km.

3 Tacey eats 144 chocolates in a competition. 60 are hard centred chocolates.
What fraction are
a hard centred chocolates
b **not** hard centred chocolates?
Simplify your answer as much as possible.

4 873 people work in a factory. 279 are men. What fraction of the total are
a men
b women?
Simplify your answer as much as possible.

10.6 Exercise B

1 Which of these is the better offer in a shop?
Offer A 'Buy two get the third half price' or
Offer B 'Buy three get the fourth free'
You **must** show your working.

2 A team consists of one goalkeeper, five defenders, three midfielders and two attackers. What fraction of the team is
a attackers
b **not** midfielders?

3 Fiona's end of year examination results were as follows.
Maths – 27 out of 40
Science – 17 out of 25
English – 14 out of 20
List the subjects in order of performance starting with the subject she did best in. You **must** show your working.

4 In a guide book there are 200 pages. 75 pages are in English, 60 pages are in French and the rest are in German. What fraction of the guidebook is
a in English
b **not** in French
c **not** in German?
Simplify your answers as much as possible.

Chapter 11

11.1 Exercise A

1 Name the following quadrilaterals.

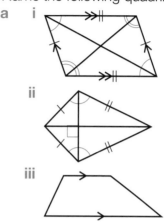

a i

ii

iii

b Name and sketch three other quadrilaterals.

2 Write down two facts about a quadrilateral.

3 Write down the letters of **two** pairs of congruent shapes from the set below.

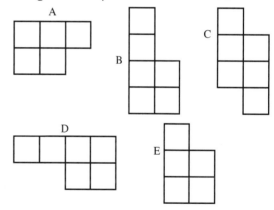

11.1 Exercise B

1 You will need to draw a grid with x and y axes labelled from 0 to 10
For each set of coordinates listed
  i draw the shape
  ii give the special name for the shape.
a (1, 1), (4, 1), (4, 2), (2, 2)
b (3, 8), (4, 5), (5, 8), (4, 9)
c (9, 3), (10, 3), (10, 7), (9, 7)
d (1, 3), (3, 3), (3, 5), (1, 5)
e (6, 9), (9, 9), (8, 10), (5, 10)

2 *PQRS* is a square.
P is the point (4, 4), *Q* is the point (6, 4) and *R* is the point (6, 6).
Find the coordinates of the point *S*.

3 The points (5, 1) and (8, 3) are two vertices of a rectangle.
Write down the coordinates of two more points which would complete the rectangle.

11.2 Exercise A

1 Write down the number of lines of symmetry of
  a a square
  b a rectangle
  c an equilateral triangle
  d an isosceles triangle
  e an isosceles trapezium
  f a parallelogram.

2 Trace the shapes and draw in any lines of symmetry.
  a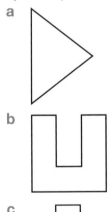
  b
  c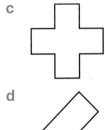
  d

3 How many lines of symmetry does each letter have?
  S   H   A   P   E

11.2 Exercise B

1 Copy each diagram onto squared paper. Draw the reflection of the shape in the mirror lines.

  a
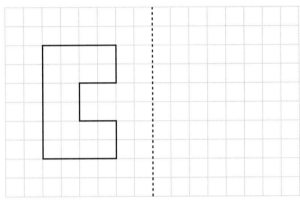

  b
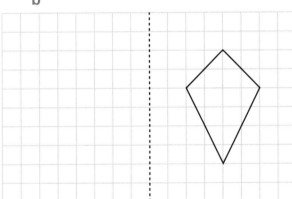

  c
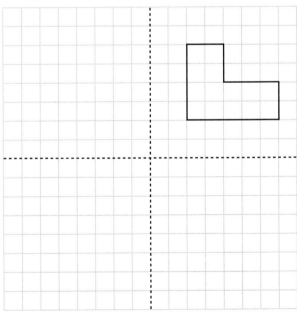

d

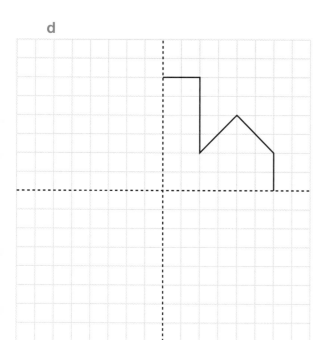

2 Make four copies of this grid

a On one copy shade four squares so that the shape has four lines of symmetry.

b On one copy shade four squares so that the shape has two lines of symmetry.

c On one copy shade four squares so that the shape has one line of symmetry.

d On one copy shade four squares so that the shape has no lines of symmetry.

11.3 Exercise A

1 What is the order of rotational symmetry for a

a square

b rhombus

c parallelogram?

2 Write down the order of rotational symmetry of these shapes.

a

b

c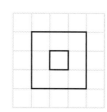

d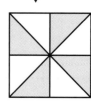

3 Which of these letters have rotational symmetry?

G   H   I   J   K

11.3 Exercise B

1 a Describe the rotational symmetry of each of the following shapes.

b Copy each shape and draw in the lines of symmetry.

i

ii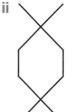

iii

2 Look at these letters

A C E H M O T X

Which letters have

a both line and rotational symmetry

b only line symmetry?

3 Shade in five more squares on the grid below to give the shape both line and rotational symmetry.

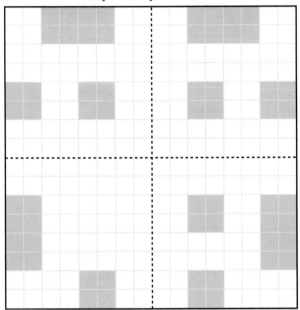

11.4 Exercise A

 1 Work out the perimeter of each shape

a
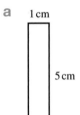

1 cm

5 cm

b
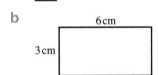

6 cm

3 cm

c
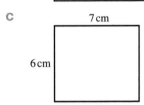

7 cm

6 cm

d
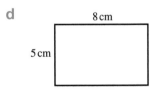

8 cm

5 cm

2 Work out the perimeter of a square with side length 8 cm.

3 Which shapes on this square grid have the same perimeter?
Show your working.

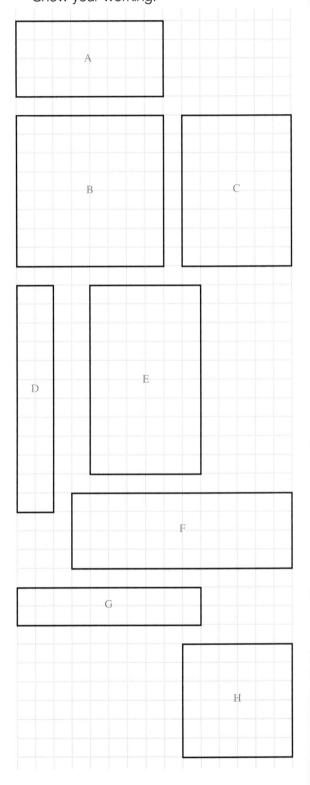

 4 Work out the perimeter of a square with side length 17.43 cm.

11.4 Exercise B

1 Work out the perimeter of each shape.

a

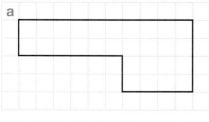

b

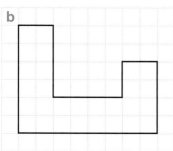

c

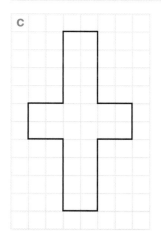

2 Calculate the perimeter of rectangles with
   a   length 8 cm and width 6 cm
   b   length 10 cm and width 9 cm.

3 The following diagrams are not drawn
   accurately. All the measurements are
   centimetres. Calculate the perimeter of
   each shape.
   All angles are right angles.

a   b   c

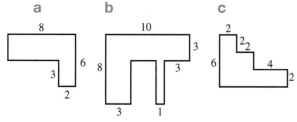

4 The perimeter of a square is 84.6 cm.
   Find the side length.

5 The length of a rectangle is 14.5 cm. The
   perimeter of the rectangle is 70 cm.
   Calculate the width of the rectangle.

11.5 Exercise A

1 Find the areas of these shapes by
   counting squares.

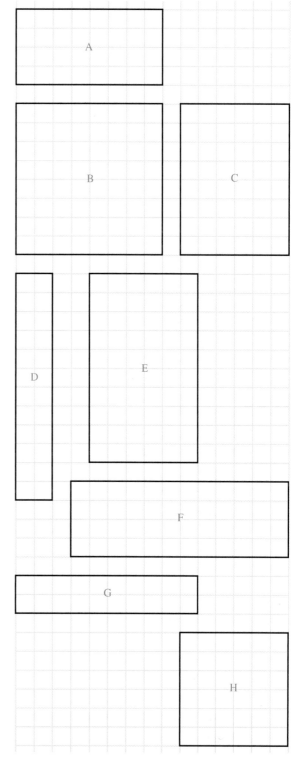

2 Find the areas of these shapes.

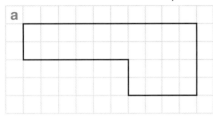

a

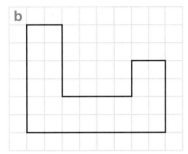

b

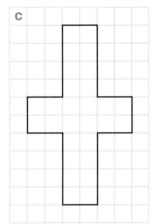

c

11.5 Exercise B

 1 Calculate the areas of these shapes. All lengths are centimetres.

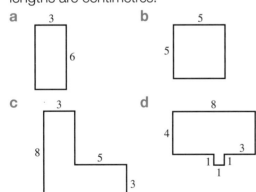

a   3

b   5

c   3   d   8

2 A kitchen floor is 5 m long and 2.5 m wide. Find the area of the kitchen floor.

3 A square has an area of 49 cm². Find the side length.

 4 Calculate the area of
   a   a football pitch 120 m long and 80 m wide
   b   a calculator 12.4 cm long and 7.1 cm wide
   c   a square tea bag 57 mm long.

5 A rectangular swimming pool is 25 m long and has an area of 550 m². How wide is the pool?

6 Rectangles A and B have the same area. Calculate the length, x, of rectangle B.

7 cm x

A   8 cm   B   4 cm

Chapter 12

12.1 Exercise A

 1 An empty box weighs 20 g. Here is a formula for working out the weight, in grams, of the contents of the box.

Weight of contents =
weight of box including contents − 20

   a   The box and its contents weigh 100 g. What is the weight of the contents?
   b   The contents of the box weigh 180 g. What is the weight of the box and its contents?

2 Mel uses this formula to work out the cost of hiring a car.

Cost of hire (in pounds) =
10 × number of hours + 25

   a   How much will it cost to hire the car for 10 hours?
   b   The car cost £95 to hire. For how many hours was it hired?

3 Jean-Francois earns £15 per hour working as a chef.
   a   Write a word formula to work out Jean-Francois's pay for any number of hours he works.

b On Friday Jean-Francois worked for 8 hours. Use the formula to work out how much Jean-Francois earned on Friday.

4 This formula can be used to find the cost of an item including VAT.

Cost including VAT = cost before VAT × 1.175

a A suit costs £250 before VAT. What is the cost of the suit including VAT?

b A van costs £9400 including VAT. What was the cost of the van before VAT?

12.1 Exercise B

1 The cost of catering for a party using 'Foodfriend' is worked out using this formula:

Cost of catering (in pounds) = 5 × number of people + 50

Kat's Katering use the formula:

Cost of catering (in pounds) = 4 × number of people + 100

Which company is cheaper to cater for
a 10 people
b 50 people
c 100 people?
You **must** show your working.

2 Three rules are suggested to connect the number of dots to the number of the rows in the triangles shown in the table

Diagram	Dots	Rows
.	1	1
. . .	3	2
. . . . . .	6	3
. . . .	10	4

Javinder's rule – to find the number of dots, double the number of rows and subtract one.

Kayleigh's rule – to find the number of dots, times the number of rows by three and subtract one.

Lori's rule – to find the number of dots, times the number of rows by the number of rows plus one and then divide by two.

a Check each rule and state whose works.

b Use the correct rule to find the number of dots in a triangle with 10 rows.

3 The takings for one stand when United play at home are calculated using the formula:

Total takings in pounds = 30 × number of adults + 15 × number of children

Calculate the total takings when there are 7143 adults and 894 children who have paid to sit in the stand.

12.2 Exercise A

1 Calculate the values of A to D when $x = 4$, $y = 5$ and $z = 10$
a $A = xy - z$
b $B = 5x - 4y$
c $C = \dfrac{xy}{z}$
d $D = \dfrac{z}{y} + \dfrac{8}{x}$

2 The formula $p = q(r + s)$ connects the quantities, p, q, r and s.
a Find p when $q = 3$, $r = 4$ and $s = 5$
b Find p when $q = 10$, $r = 20$ and $s = 30$
c Find q when $p = 45$, $r = 3$ and $s = 6$

3 a A window cleaner charges 30 pence for each window he cleans. Write down a formula for p pence, the cost of cleaning w windows.
b Jeff buys a apples at 10 pence each, and b bananas at 20 pence each. Write down a formula for t, the total cost of the fruit.
c An isosceles triangle has sides of length x and $2x$. Write down two possible formulae for the perimeter, P, of the isosceles triangle.

12.2 Exercise B

1 Use $a = -2$, $b = 3$, $c = -4$ and $d = 5$ to calculate the values of A to D in the formulae below.

a $A = c - 2a$ b $B = 5d - c^2$

c $C = (b + c + d)^3$

d $D = ab + bc + cd$

2 In a tea room tea costs 35 pence a cup and a scone is 45 pence.

a i Write down an expression for the cost of x cups of tea.

  ii Write down an expression for the cost of y scones.

b Write down a formula for t, the total cost in pence of x cups of tea and y scones.

c A family of four spent £2.75. Each person had a cup of tea. How many scones were bought?

3 a $A = c^2 - 3c$ Find A when $c = 22$

b $Q = 5g^2 - g^3$ Find Q when $g = 9$

c $T = spg$ Find T when $s = 7$, $p = 10$ and $g = 13$

d $L = w + \dfrac{r}{z}$ Find w when $L = 20$, $r = 6$ and $z = 30$

4 A carpenter earns a weekly wage of £P for working H hours in a week. The carpenter's weekly wage is worked out using the formula $P = 8H + 50$

a In the first week in November the carpenter works for 35 hours. Work out the carpenter's weekly wage for the first week in November.

b In the second week in November the carpenter earns £370. How many hours did the carpenter work in the second week in November?

Chapter 13

13.1 Exercise A

1 Write down the mode for each list. There could be more than one mode, or no mode at all.

a 4 7 3 6 2 7

b 16 14 13 13 12 14

c 1 2 3 4 5 6 7

d 0.6 0.2 0.4 0.8 0.3 0.1 0.9 0.9

2 Write down the modal item from each list.

a cat dog rabbit fish dog cat dog hamster

b score miss miss miss score miss score

c A B A C D B C A C

d PG 12 U 18 15 12 U PG 12

3 Work out the calculations. Which is the modal answer?

$7 + 8$, 2×7, 4^2, 8×2, 14×1, $20 - 5$, $18 - 2$, $32 \div 2$, $18 - 6 + 2$, $2 + 3 \times 2$

13.1 Exercise B

1

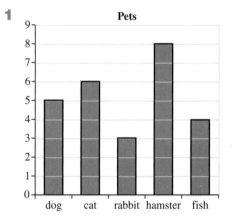

Pets

Use the bar chart to find the modal type of pet.

2 The frequency table shows the type of goal scored by a team in one season.

Type of goal	Frequency
Header	12
Penalty	4
Shot from outside box	8
Shot from inside box	29
Own goal	2

What was the modal type of goal scored?

3 Write a list of six numbers which have a mode of 10

4 Write a list of eight numbers with modes of 7 and 8

13.2 Exercise A

1 Calculate the mean for each set of numbers
  a 7 10 6 5
  b 8 3 9 4 6
  c 25 45 30 60 15 75 30
  d 7 2 4 1 9 3 2 8 5 6

2 Brandy asked 10 of her friends how many cats they had ever owned.
Their replies were

2 0 3 8 2 1 1 0 3 3
  a Find the mean number of cats owned by Brandy's friends.
  b Is the mean greater than the mode? Explain your answer.

3 What is the mean number of letters in the names of the seven days of the week?

4 Five children took part in a long jump competition.
Their best jumps were 3.24 m, 2.96 m, 4.08 m, 3.73 m and 4.19 m.
  a Calculate the mean length of long jump.
  b How many jumped longer than the mean?

13.2 Exercise B

1 8 data values have a total of 160. What is their mean?

2 5 data values have a mean of 6. What is their total?

3 Suzy's sandwich bar sells sandwiches on either white or brown rolls. The following table shows the number of each type sold over five days.

Day	number of white	number of brown
M	8	12
Tu	10	10
W	7	11
Th	15	13
F	10	14

Compare the mean number of sandwiches sold on white rolls with the mean number sold on brown rolls.

4 The mean of 8 numbers is 345
7 of the numbers are 301, 382, 297, 284, 453, 347 and 381
Find the 8th number.

5 Write down a list of 6 numbers with mode 5 and mean 7

13.3 Exercise A

1 Write down the median of each data set
  a 3 4 6 7 8
  b 10 8 5 1 0
  c 3 9 2 8 6 3 5
  d −9 −1 4 −2 9 −3 2 1 −7

2 The numbers of students in each Year 7 form at Michelle's school are:
28 29 29 27 28 30 27 28 27
Find the median number of students in each form.

3 The time (in seconds) for nine students to finish a 100 metre race was as follows:
12.9 13.3 12.8 13.1 14.6 13.1 12.5 11.7 12.0
Find the median finishing time.

13.3 Exercise B

1 Calculate the median of each data set.
  a 3 4 6 8
  b 9 7 3 2 1 0
  c 7 3 2 9 6 7 1 2 1 2
  d 30 −20 −80 60 40 90

2 Bill asks his friends how many calls they received on their mobiles that day. Their replies were:

4   0   2   18   3   2   9   10

Find the median number of calls.

3 **a** Write down three numbers with a median of 10

   b Write down four numbers with a median of 5

   c Write down five different numbers with a median of 0

   d Write down four numbers with a median of 2 and a mean of 3

   e Write down nine numbers with a median of 7, a mean of 9 and a mode of 6

13.4 Exercise A

1 Calculate the range of each set of data.

   a 3   4   7   12   13   21

   b 0   22   45   57   134   233

   c −3   0   4   8   12   23

   d −11   −9   −8   −4   −2

   e 34   21   8   −4   0   23

   f 9   23   51   −23   44   −30   5

2 The number of DVDs owned by five friends is

22   3   67   26   50

Find the range of the number of DVDs owned by the friends.

3 The highest temperature each day for a week in a holiday resort was

32   31   33   30   39   29   41

Find the range of these temperatures.

4 The time (in seconds) for nine students to finish a 100 metre race was as follows:

12.9   13.3   12.8   13.1   14.6   13.1   12.5   11.7   12.0

Find the range of the finishing times.

13.4 Exercise B

1 The bar chart shows the number of patients seen by each of four doctors in one morning.

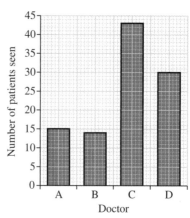

   a How many patients were seen by Doctor A?

   b Which doctor saw the most patients?

   c Calculate the range of the number of patients seen.

2 Students were asked how they travelled to college.

The bar chart shows the results.

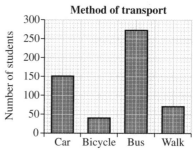

Find the range of the number of students who used each method of transport.

3 The number of cars caught speeding each day on a certain road is shown in the pictogram.

   a How many cars were caught speeding on Monday?

   b On which day were the least number of cars caught speeding?

   c Calculate the range of the number of cars that were speeding on the days represented by the pictogram.

4 The pictogram shows the number of houses with the number of telephones in each house.

Key 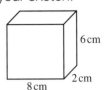 = 2 houses

Number of telephones	Number of houses
0	🕾 🕾
1	🕾 🕾 🕾 🕾
2	🕾 🕾 🕾
3	🕾 🕾
4	🕾

a Calculate the range of the number of houses.

b Calculate the range of the number of telephones.

Chapter 14

14.1 Exercise A

1 For each of the three-dimensional shapes listed

  a draw a sketch of the shape

  b write down the number of

    i faces

    ii edges

    iii vertices

  A cuboid   **B** square based pyramid

  C cube   **D** tetrahedron

  E triangular prism   **F** sphere

2 Write down an object you have seen today which is in the shape of

  a a sphere   **b** a cuboid

  c a cylinder   **d** a cone

14.1 Exercise B

1 State whether each of these statements is true or false.

  a The net of a cube is made up of six squares.

  b The net of a cuboid has to be made up of six rectangles.

  c The net of a tetrahedron is made up of four triangles.

2 Sketch three different nets which will make a cube.

3 Sketch a net of each of these solids. Label all the lengths on your sketch.

  a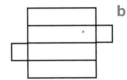

  b

  c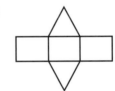

4 Name and sketch the solid which can be made from each of these nets.

  a   **b**

  c

14.2 Exercise A

1 These shapes are made from one centimetre cubes.
Find the volume of each shape.

  a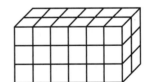

  b

  c

  d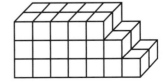

2 Calculate the volume of these cubes and cuboids.
State the units in your answers.

a
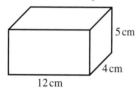

b
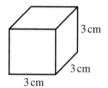

c
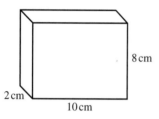

d
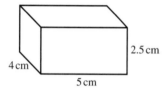

 3 The table gives the measurements of three cuboids. Calculate the volumes.

Cuboid	Length (cm)	Width (cm)	Height (cm)	Volume (cm³)
a	3.5	2.5	1.5	
b	15	12	9	
c	8.7	3.9	3.9	

4 A shoe box is in the shape of a cuboid.
The box is 32.7 cm long, 13.9 cm wide and 9.7 cm high.
Calculate the volume of the shoe box.

14.2 Exercise B

 1 Calculate the heights of these cuboids

a
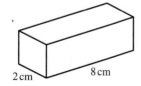
Volume 48 cm³

b
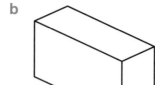
Volume 42 cm³

c
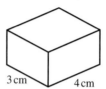
Volume 60 cm³

d
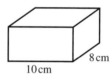
Volume 800 cm³

2 Use the formula $V = l \times w \times h$ to find
   a V when $l = 2$ cm, $w = 1.5$ cm, $h = 1$ cm
   b l when $w = 4$ cm, $h = 2$ cm, $V = 16$ cm³
   c w when $l = 5$ cm, $h = 3$ cm, $V = 45$ cm³
   d h when $l = 10$ m, $w = 5$ m, $V = 300$ m³

 3 A cuboid shaped box is 7.9 cm long, 5.5 cm wide and 14.7 cm high. It is $\frac{3}{4}$ full of flour. Calculate the volume of
   a the box
   b the flour
   c the part of the box without flour.

Chapter 15

15.1 Exercise A

 1 For each of these sequences
   i give the term-to-term rule
   ii write down the next three terms.
   a 3, 5, 7, 9, …   **b** 3, 6, 12, 24,…
   c 8000, 4000, 2000, 1000, …
   d 30, 21, 12, 3, …
   e −13, −10, −7, −4, …
   f 30 000, 3000, 300, 30, …

2 Some of the terms are missing in these sequences. Find the missing terms.
- a   ..., ..., 8, 11, ..., ..., 20
- b   ..., ..., 1, 9, ..., 25, 33
- c   24, ..., 18, ..., ..., 9, ...
- d   10 000, 2000, ..., ..., 16, ...

3 The first term of a sequence of numbers is 6. The rule for continuing the sequence is **divide by −2**
Write down the first three terms of the sequence.

4 The term-to-term rule for a sequence is **add 4.** The first term is −7
Find the fourth term.

15.1 Exercise B

1 For each of these sequences
- i   describe in words the differences between consecutive terms of the sequence
- ii write down the next three terms.
- a   2, 3, 5, 8, 12, ...
- b   1, 5, 13, 25, ...
- c   20, 19, 17, 14, 10, ...
- d   −20, −17, −12, −5, ...

2 a   The second term of a sequence of numbers is 20
The rule for continuing the sequence is **multiply by 3 then add 2**
Write down the first five terms of the sequence.
- b   The second term of a sequence of numbers is 120
The rule for continuing the sequence is **divide by 2 then subtract 4**
Write down the first three terms of the sequence.

3 Use the number patterns to complete each of the following
- a $1 \times 999 = 999$
$2 \times 999 = 1998$
$3 \times 999 = 2997$
$4 \times 999 = ...$
$5 \times 999 = ...$

- b $101 \times 22 = 2222$
$101 \times 222 = 22\ 422$
$101 \times 2222 = 224\ 422$
$101 \times 22\ 222 = ...$
$101 \times 222\ 222 = ...$

4 Find the missing terms in each sequence.
- a   5, 8, 13, ..., 29, ...
- b   ..., ..., 7, 4, 0, ..., ...

15.2 Exercise A

1 Matchsticks are used to make this sequence of patterns.

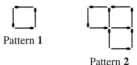

Pattern **1**

Pattern **2**

Pattern **3**

- a   Draw pattern 4
- b   What is the term-to-term rule for the sequence of the number of matchsticks in each pattern?
- c   Complete the table to show the number of matchsticks in each pattern.

Pattern number	1	2	3	4	5	10
Number of matchsticks	4	10	16			

- d   Which pattern uses 124 matchsticks?

2 Here are the first three patterns in a sequence of dot patterns.

Pattern **1**   Pattern **2**   Pattern **3**

- a   Draw pattern 4
- b   Complete the table to show the number of dots in each pattern.

Pattern number	1	2	3	4
Number of dots				

- c   What is the term-to-term rule for the sequence made up of the number of dots in each pattern?
- d   How many dots are there in
  - i   pattern 10
  - ii pattern 100?

3 This sequence of pentagon patterns is made from matchsticks.

a How many matchsticks are needed to make four pentagons?

b Copy and complete the table to show the number of matchsticks in each pattern.

Number of pentagons	1	2	3	4	5
Number of matchsticks	5				

c How many **more** matchsticks are needed to make the pattern with six pentagons from the pattern with five pentagons?

d How many matchsticks are needed to make ten pentagons?

e How many pentagons can be made with 61 matchsticks?

15.2 Exercise B

1 This pattern is made from dots.

a Draw the next two patterns in the sequence.

b Copy and complete this table.

Pattern			Number of dots
1	1	$\frac{1 \times 2}{2}$	1
2	1 + 2	$\frac{2 \times 3}{2}$	3
3	1 + 2 + 3	$\frac{3 \times 4}{2}$	6
4	1 + 2 + 3 + 4	$\frac{4 \times 5}{2}$	10
5			
6			

c How many dots are there in pattern
  i 9   ii 99?

d Which pattern has 5050 matchsticks?

e Work out 1 + 2 + 3 + ... + 1000

2 The table shows sequences of squares made from matchsticks.

a Copy the table and extend it to patterns of height 4 and width 4

Height of pattern (h)	Width of pattern (w)		
	1	2	3
1			
2			
3			

b Copy and complete this table.

h	w				Term-to-term rule
	1	2	3	4	
1	4	7	10		Add 3
2	7	12	17		
3	10	17	24		
4					
5					
10					

c This table shows the formulae for working out the number of matchsticks needed to make patterns for different values of height h and width w.

h	Formula
1	$m = 3w + 1$
2	$m = 5w + 2$
3	$m = 7w + 3$
4	$m = 9w + 4$

i A pattern has $h = 3$ and $w = 10$
How many matchsticks does this pattern use?

ii A pattern uses 85 matchsticks and has width 9
What is its height?

iii Find the formula when $h = 5$

iv Find the formula when $h = 10$

Chapter 16

16.1 Exercise A

1 Describe the chance of each event happening. Choose from these words.

> impossible   unlikely   even chance
> likely   certain

a You will eat ice cream next summer.

b A pigeon will be the next Prime Minister.

c It will rain somewhere in the world tomorrow.

d A fair coin will land on tails when flipped.

2 Write down an event about the weather which is

a impossible   b certain

c unlikely   d likely

3 A box contains 100 coloured balls.
Half of the balls are red, 30 are blue and 20 are green.
A ball is picked without looking.
Describe the chance of the following events.

a The ball picked is red.

b The ball picked is blue.

c The ball picked is **not** green.

d The ball picked is yellow.

16.1 Exercise B

1 Neal has a set of cards, 10 are blue, 5 are red and 5 are green.
Barry has a similar set but 8 are blue, 1 is red and 1 is green.
If they both pick a card, who is more likely to pick a blue card?
Explain your answer.

2 Amy spins a triangular spinner.

Ray rolls an ordinary dice.
Amy says that she has more chance of getting a '1' than Ray has of getting a '1'.
Is she correct? Explain your answer.

3 Jarnail buys 10 raffle tickets each month for a year.
Mo buys 100 tickets per year for the same raffle.
Who is more likely to win a prize when the raffle is drawn at the end of the year?
Explain your answer.

16.2 Exercise A

All coins and dice in this exercise are fair unless otherwise stated.

1 Copy this probability scale.
Show the probability of each of the following events on the scale.

a A coin is flipped and it lands showing tails.

b A six-sided dice is rolled and it shows the number 5

c A coin is flipped and shows the number 3

d A six-sided dice is rolled and it shows a number.

2 There are ten coloured discs in a bag, five are yellow, three are red and two are blue.
A disc is pulled from the bag without looking.
Copy this probability scale.
Label the probability of each event on the probability scale.

```
├──┼──┼──┼──┼──┼──┼──┼──┼──┼──┤
0                              1
```

a The disc is yellow.

b The disc is red.

c The disc is blue.

d The disc is black.

3 A fair dice is thrown. Mark the probabilities of each of the following events on a probability scale.

a The dice shows the number 4

b The dice shows an even number.

c The dice shows the number 0

d The dice shows the number 1 or more.

16.2 Exercise B

1 The probabilities of the following events have been marked on the probability scale.

   a The next person to get off a bus will be a 15 year old girl.

   b You have used a computer in the last year.

   c If the hands of a clock are showing 12 o'clock it is midnight.

0   1

   Copy the scale and label each arrow with a letter to show which event it represents.

2 A large field contains 30 white sheep, 20 black sheep, 100 black and white cows and 50 brown cows. One animal escapes.
   On a probability scale label the following probabilities.

   a The animal that escapes is a white sheep.

   b The animal that escapes is a black and white cow.

   c The animal that escapes is a sheep

   d The animal that escapes is not brown.

3 A bag of coloured discs contains 10 blue, 15 red, 55 green and 20 purple discs.
   A disc is picked from the bag without looking.

   a Work out the probability of picking

      i a blue disc

      ii a red disc

      iii a green disc

      iv an orange disc.

   b Draw a probability scale and label it to show these probabilities.

4 Work out the probability of a fair 8-sided dice showing

   a   **i** 5   **ii** more than 4

       iii 3 or less   **iv** 9 or 10

   b Show each of the probabilities **i** to **iv** on a probability scale.

16.3 Exercise A

1 List all the possible outcomes for each event.

   a Rolling a dice numbered 1 to 6

   b Picking one disc from a bag containing red, blue and green discs.

   c Choosing a day of the week at random.

   d Choosing a coin from a bottle of British coins.

2 An 8-sided dice has four faces labelled 'D', two labelled 'I', one labelled 'C' and one labelled 'E'.
   The dice is rolled.

   a List all the possible outcomes

   b Explain why each outcome is not equally likely.

3 The letters of the word PROBABILITY are each written onto separate cards and placed inside a bag.
   Anders picks one letter from the bag.

   a List all the possible outcomes for the letter Anders picks.

   b Which letters are more likely to be chosen?

   c Write down an outcome that is impossible.

4 A fair 6-sided dice has its faces labelled with C H A N C E.
   List the possible outcomes when the dice is thrown.

16.3 Exercise B

1 Sandra buys a hot drink and a snack from a café.
   She chooses a drink from tea (T), coffee (C) and hot chocolate (H).
   She chooses a snack from a scone (S), a packet of crisps (P) and biscuits (B).
   List all the possible combinations of drink and snack that Sandra could have bought.

2 Roger buys a shirt and a tie.
Both are available as plain (P) or with checks (C), stripes (S) or dotted (D).
List all the possible combinations of patterns of shirt and tie that Roger could have bought.

3 An ordinary dice is rolled twice.
The numbers on the dice are **multiplied** to give a score.

a Copy and complete the table to show all the possible scores.

First throw

×	1	2	3	4	5	6
1	1	2				
2						
3						
4						
5						
6						36

(Second throw)

b How many different scores are possible?

c What is the most likely score?

d Explain why the score '36' is not the least likely score.

16.4 Exercise A

1 An ordinary dice is thrown.
Write down the probability that the dice lands on the number

a 3   **b** 8

c 1, 2 or 3   **d** 6 or less

2 A fair spinner has 10 sections numbered
1, 1, 1, 1, 2, 2, 2, 3, 3, 4
Write down the probability that the spinner lands on a section numbered

a 1   **b** 2

c 3 or 4   **d** 5 or 6

3 Dale is trying to choose a number between 1 and 49 (inclusive) at random. What is the probability that if he does choose at random he will choose

a 34   **b** 48 or 49

c an odd number

d a number ending in 7

e a square number

f a prime number?

16.4 Exercise B

1 This dice is thrown and the spinner is spun. The number on the dice and the number on the spinner are multiplied to give a score.

a Make a table of all the possible outcomes for the score.

b Calculate the probability of a score of

  i 10

  ii 12

  iii 13

  iv an odd number.

2 An 8-sided dice numbered 1 to 8 is thrown twice. The numbers that the dice show are added to give a score.

a Make a table of all the possible outcomes for the score.

b Calculate the probability of a score of

  i 8

  ii 9

  iii an even number

  iv a square number.

3 The probability that the first piece of luggage out of an aeroplane and onto the conveyor belt is Basil's is $\frac{1}{150}$. How many pieces of luggage were on the plane altogether if Basil had

a one piece of luggage

b two pieces of luggage?

4 A disc is red (R) on one side and blue (B) on the other side.
The disc is flipped three times and the colour recorded.
RRR is one possible outcome.
List the other seven possible outcomes.

16.5 Exercise A

1 A bag contains 10 discs.
   The discs are numbered 1 to 10
   A disc is chosen at random from the bag.
   a List the possible outcomes for the
     number on the chosen disc.
   b Are the outcomes mutually exclusive?
     Explain your answer.

2 The probability that a fair spinner lands on
   white is 0.3. What is the probability that
   the spinner does **not** land on white?

3 The probability that Wayne scores in a
   football match is 0.55. What is the
   probability that Wayne does **not** score in
   a football match?

4 The table shows some of the probabilities
   for a biased spinner.

Number	Probability
1	0.4
2	0.5
3	x

   a Find x.
   b Explain why the scores are mutually
     exclusive.

16.5 Exercise B

1 A 4-sided spinner numbered 1, 2, 3, 4 is
   spun twice.
   The numbers that the spinner lands on
   are **added** to give a score.
   a Copy and complete the following table.

+	1	2	3	4
1				
2				
3			6	
4				

   b Calculate the probability that the score
     is
     i 5   ii **not** 5

2 A fair six-sided dice and a coin are thrown.
   If the coin shows heads, the score is one
   more than the number shown on the dice.
   If the coin shows tails, the score is three
   times the number shown on the dice.
   a Copy and complete this table

	1	2	3	4	5	6
H			4			
T					15	

   b Calculate the probability that the score
     is
     i 18   ii **not** 18
     iii 3   iv **not** 3

3 The table shows some of the probabilities
   of the number of people in cars   passing
   a police car.

Number of people in car	1	2	3	4+
Probability	0.56	0.31	0.11	

   a Calculate the probability that the
     number of people in a car is
     i 3 or less   ii 4+
   b What is the most likely number of
     people in a car?

4 A 10-sided dice is numbered 1–10
   The probability that the score on this dice
   is even is 0.5
   The probability that the score on this dice
   is more than 4 is 0.6
   Jimmy says that the probability of the
   score being even or more than 4 is found
   by adding 0.5 and 0.6 to get 1.1
   a Give **two** reasons why Jimmy could
     not be correct.
   b Work out the correct answer.

Chapter 17

17.1 Exercise A

1 Work out
   a $\frac{3}{11} + \frac{4}{11}$ b $\frac{2}{9} + \frac{5}{9}$ c $\frac{10}{13} - \frac{6}{13}$
   d $\frac{4}{5} - \frac{3}{5}$ e $\frac{7}{8} - \frac{3}{4}$ f $\frac{7}{16} + \frac{1}{4}$
   g $\frac{9}{10} - \frac{3}{5}$ h $\frac{3}{11} + \frac{5}{22}$

2 Work out

  a $\frac{1}{2} + \frac{1}{3}$ **b** $\frac{1}{8} + \frac{1}{3}$

  c $\frac{1}{5} - \frac{1}{6}$ **d** $\frac{4}{7} - \frac{1}{3}$

3 Work out these calculations. Simplify your answers if possible.

  a $\frac{5}{12} + \frac{5}{12}$ **b** $\frac{7}{15} - \frac{2}{5}$

  c $\frac{9}{10} - \frac{2}{5}$ **d** $\frac{4}{21} + \frac{2}{7}$

4 Copy these rectangles.
Shade in the rectangles to complete the subtraction.

$$\frac{3}{4} \quad - \quad \frac{1}{6} \quad = \quad \ldots\ldots\ldots\ldots$$

5 Use a calculator to check your answers to questions **1** to **4**

17.1 Exercise B

1 Work out the following. Give your answers as mixed numbers where necessary.

  a $1\frac{1}{3} + 1\frac{1}{4}$ **b** $2\frac{2}{5} - 1\frac{1}{10}$

  c $3\frac{2}{9} + 5\frac{1}{6}$ **d** $6\frac{2}{3} - 3\frac{1}{8}$

2 A bucket holds $4\frac{2}{3}$ litres of water when full. If $2\frac{5}{7}$ litres of water are poured into the empty bucket, how many more litres of water would be needed to fill the bucket?

3 A pair of twins weigh $5\frac{1}{4}$ and $4\frac{7}{8}$ pounds respectively. What is the total weight of the pair of twins?

4 Use your calculator to check your answers to questions **1** to **3**

17.2 Exercise A

1 Work out the following, leaving each answer as an integer or a mixed number as appropriate.

  a $\frac{1}{3} \times 9$ **b** $\frac{1}{6} \times 7$

  c $\frac{1}{8} \times 32$ **d** $\frac{1}{10} \times 25$

2 Work out the following, leaving each answer as a proper fraction.

  a $\frac{1}{3} \times \frac{1}{5}$ **b** $\frac{1}{7} \times \frac{1}{2}$

  c $\frac{2}{5} \times \frac{3}{7}$ **d** $\frac{7}{11} \times \frac{1}{10}$

3 Work out the following, giving each answer as a proper fraction in its simplest form.

  a $\frac{2}{5} \times \frac{1}{6}$ **b** $\frac{3}{4} \times \frac{2}{9}$

  c $\frac{4}{11} \times \frac{11}{100}$ **d** $\frac{8}{15} \times \frac{5}{16}$

4 Use your calculator to check your answers to questions **1** to **3**

17.2 Exercise B

1 Work out the following, leaving your answer as a proper fraction or an integer as appropriate.

  a $\frac{1}{5} \div 2$ **b** $\frac{1}{7} \div 10$

  c $\frac{1}{5} \div \frac{1}{10}$ **d** $\frac{1}{8} \div \frac{1}{24}$

2 Work out these division calculations, giving each answer as a mixed number.

  a $\frac{1}{3} \div \frac{1}{4}$ **b** $\frac{2}{3} \div \frac{1}{8}$

  c $\frac{1}{8} \div \frac{1}{20}$ **d** $\frac{5}{8} \div \frac{2}{5}$

3 Work out these division calculations, giving each answer as a proper fraction in its simplest form.

  a $\frac{2}{3} \div \frac{5}{9}$ **b** $\frac{5}{12} \div \frac{7}{12}$

  c $\frac{1}{10} \div \frac{3}{4}$ **d** $\frac{2}{9} \div \frac{1}{15}$

4 Use your calculator to check your answers to questions **1** to **3**

17.3 Exercise A

1 Work out

  a $0.2 + 0.4$

  b $1.6 + 3.1$

  c $21.4 + 16.5$

  d $0.38 + 0.61$

  e $0.9 - 0.5$

  f $7.9 - 6.3$

  g $54.3 - 32.1$

  h $85.6 - 44.6$

2 Work out
  a   0.54 + 0.67
  b   6.24 + 7.19
  c   84.67 + 77.38
  d   814.65 + 77.68
  e   2.8 − 1.9
  f   51.3 − 28.7
  g   24.56 − 18.87
  h   61.54 − 56.56

3 Work out
  a   25.647 + 36.978
  b   54.14 − 26.98
  c   4705.3 + 256.9
  d   4705.3 − 256.9

 4 Use your calculator to check your answers to questions **1** to **3**

17.3 Exercise B

 1 Find the missing values
  a   0.5 + ... = 0.8
  b   2.4 + ... = 4.9
  c   54.81 + ... = 79.86
  d   91.41 + ... = 197.69
  e   ..... + 45.3 = 59.6
  f   32.8 + ... = 54.1
  g   ..... + 32.47 = 51.18
  h   1.236 + ... = 2.123

2 Find the missing values
  a   0.9 − ..... = 0.1
  b   ..... − 0.5 = 1.1
  c   12.5 − ..... = 7.1
  d   ..... − 23.6 = 88.4
  e   0.13 + 0.69 + ... = 2.22
  f   ..... + 23.45 + 26.58 = 67.45
  g   ..... + 6.3 − 4.1 = 12.1
  h   48.56 − 24.67 = ... + 19.14

3 Work out
  a   1.5 − 0.41
  b   6.5 − 3.88
  c   36.2 − 17.8
  d   239 − 65.2

 4 Use your calculator to check your answers to questions **1** to **3**

Chapter 18

18.1 Exercise A

 1 Write down the coordinates of points A to J on this diagram.

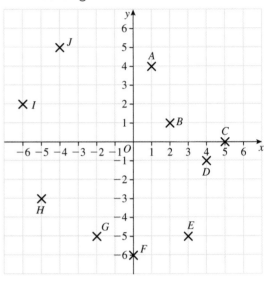

2 Make a blank copy of the grid from question **1**
On the grid draw and label the points $K(3, 1)$, $L(6, 2)$, $M(4, -2)$, $N(0, 5)$, $P(-2, 3)$, $Q(-5, 0)$, $R(-2, -3)$, $S(-6, -1)$ and $T(2, -6)$.

3 Draw a grid with both the x-axis and the y-axis from −5 to 5
  a   Plot the points $(-3, -5)$ and $(2, 5)$. Join them with a straight line.
  b   Plot the points $(-5, 3)$ and $(1, -3)$. Join them with a straight line.
  c   Write down the coordinates of the point where the two lines cross.

18.1 Exercise B

 1 Draw a coordinate grid with both the x-axis and the y-axis from 0 to 6
  a   i   Plot five coordinates with an x-coordinate of 6 in one colour.
      ii Plot five coordinates with a y-coordinate of 5 in a second colour.
      iii Plot five coordinates where the x-coordinate is one more than the y-coordinate in a third colour.

b Look at the sets of points you plotted in part **a**. What do you notice?

2 In this set of coordinates the y-coordinates are missing.

$$(-2, ?), (-1, ?), (0, ?),$$
$$(1, ?), (2, ?), (3, ?)$$

The x- and y-coordinates are connected by this rule.

y-coordinate $= 2 \times x$-coordinate -1

a Work out the missing y-coordinates.

b Plot the completed coordinates on a coordinate diagram.

c What do you notice about these points?

3 a Match each point to one of the descriptions.

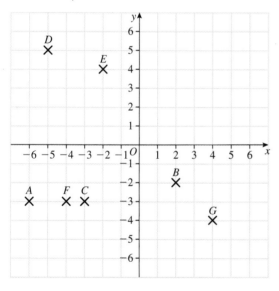

i The y-coordinate equals -4

ii The y-coordinate equals the x-coordinate plus 1

iii The y-coordinate equals the x-coordinate minus 4

iv The y-coordinate is half the x-coordinate.

v The x-coordinate equals -2

b Two points do **not** have a description.
Write a description for each of these points.

4 A sequence of coordinates starts with the point $(-5, 7)$. The term-to-term rules for continuing the sequence are:

x-coordinate | Add 1 |

y-coordinate | Subtract 3 |

a Write down the first five coordinates in the sequence.

b Plot the coordinates on a coordinate diagram with the x-axis from -6 to 1 and the y-axis from -6 to 8

c What do you notice?

18.2 Exercise A

1 For each table draw a grid with both the x-axis and the y-axis from 0 to 12 then

  i find the rule connecting each x- coordinate with each y-coordinate

  ii write a list of coordinates from the table and plot them on the grid

  iii draw and label the line through the plotted points.

a

x	0	1	2	3	4	5
y	0	2	4	6	8	10

b

x	0	1	2	3	4	5
y	3	4	5	6	7	8

c

x	0	1	2	3	4	5
y	2	4	6	8	10	12

2 On a grid with both the x-axis and y-axis from 0 to 10, draw the lines

  a $x = 2$ **b** $y = 5$

  c $x = 8$ **d** $y = 7$

3 a **i** Complete this table for $y = 2x + 1$

x	-2	-1	0	1	2
y	-3	-1	1		

  ii Draw the graph of $y = 2x + 1$

 b **i** Complete this table $y = 4x + 1$

x	-2	-1	0	1	2
y	-7	-3			

  ii Draw the graph of $y = 4x + 1$

c **i** Complete this table for $y = 3 - x$

x	−1	0	1	2	3	4
y				1		

    ii Draw the graph of $y = 3 - x$.

18.2 Exercise B

1 **a** Copy and complete the table for
$y = 4x - 3$

x	−2	−1	0	1	2	3
y						

  b **i** Draw a grid with the x-axis from −3
to 4 and the y-axis from −12 to 10
    ii On the grid draw the graph of
$y = 4x - 3$
  c Use the graph to find the value of y
when $x = -1.5$
  d Use the graph to find the value of x
when $y = 0.5$

2 **a** **i** Copy and complete the following
table for $x + y = 8$

x	0	2	5	8
y				

    ii Copy and complete the following
table for $x + y = 12$

x	0	3	7	12
y				

  b Draw a grid with both the x-axis and
the y-axis from 0 to 12
  c Draw the lines $x + y = 8$ and
$x + y = 12$ on the grid.

3 **a** Draw a grid with x-axis from −1 to 6
and y-axis from −5 to 12
  b The coordinates $(0, -4)$, $(2, 2)$ and
$(5, 11)$ lie on the graph of $y = 3x - 4$
Draw the graph of $y = 3x - 4$
  c Find the coordinates of the point
where $y = 3x - 4$ meets
    i the line $y = x$
    ii the line $y = 2x + 1$

Chapter 19

19.1 Exercise A

1 For each shape
  i copy the shape and the mirror line
onto squared paper
  ii draw the image of the shape after
reflection in the mirror line.

a

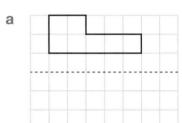

b

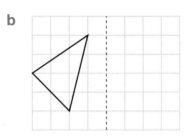

c

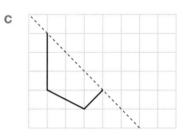

d

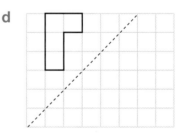

2 For each shape
  i copy the axes and the shape onto
squared paper
  ii draw the image of the shape after
reflection in the x-axis
  iii draw the image of the original shape
after reflection in the y-axis.

a

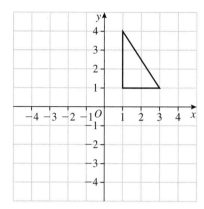

b

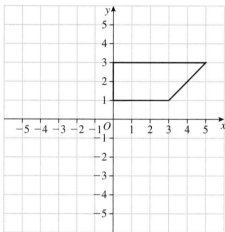

c

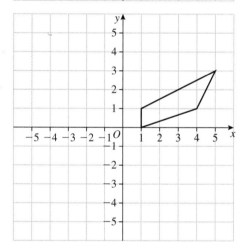

d

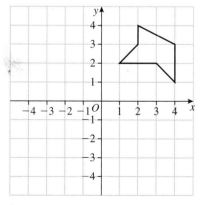

19.1 Exercise B

1 Draw x and y-axes from -4 to $+10$ on a grid.
Copy triangle A onto your grid.

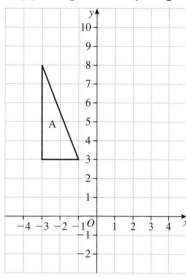

Draw the reflection of triangle A in the lines
a $x = 1$ **b** $y = 2$ **c** $x = y$

2 Draw x and y-axes from -7 to $+7$ on a grid.
Copy shape B onto your grid.

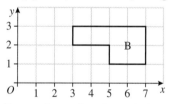

Draw the reflection of shape B in the lines
a $x = 0$ **b** $y = -1$ **c** $x = -y$

3

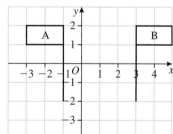

a Describe the single transformation which moves flag A to flag B.
b Describe the single transformation which moves flag B to flag A.
c What do you notice about your answers to parts **a** and **b**?

19.2 Exercise A

1 Copy each diagram onto squared paper
   i draw the enlargement of each shape
     by scale factor 2
   ii draw the enlargement of each shape
     by scale factor 3

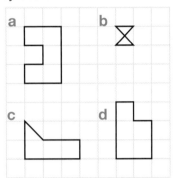

a   b

c   d

2 For the shape in part **d** of question **1**
   a find the perimeter of the original shape
   b find the perimeter of the enlargement
     by scale factor 2
   c what do you notice about the
     perimeters of the two shapes and the
     scale factor?

19.2 Exercise B

1 Enlarge the triangle
   by scale factor 2
   with centre of
   enlargement (0, 0)

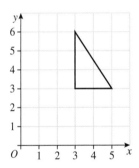

2 Enlarge each of the following diagrams
   using the given scale factor and centre of
   enlargement.
   a Scale factor 3, centre of enlargement
     (4, 0)

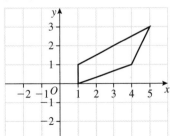

b Scale factor $\frac{1}{2}$,
   centre of
   enlargement
   (−1, 1)

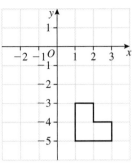

c Scale factor 2, centre of enlargement
   (6, 4)

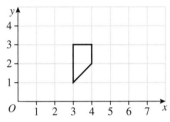

d Scale factor $\frac{1}{3}$, centre of enlargement
   (7, 1)

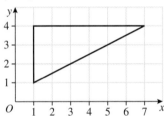

3 Describe fully the single transformation
   that transforms
   a shape A to shape B
   b shape B to shape A

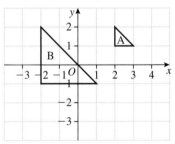

4 a i Enlarge this shape
       by a scale factor
       of 2
     ii How many times
       bigger is the area of
       the enlarged shape
       than the area of the small shape?

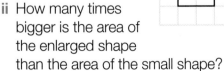

b Repeat part **a** for a scale factor of 3

c Predict how many times bigger the area of a shape will be after it has been enlarged by a scale factor of 4 Test your prediction.

19.3 Exercise A

1 Copy and complete the following sentences.

   a A rotation of 270 degrees clockwise is equivalent to a rotation of … degrees anticlockwise.

   b A half turn is equal to … degrees.

   c 45 degrees is equal to one … of a turn.

   d A rotation of 250 degrees clockwise followed by a rotation of 80 degrees anticlockwise is equivalent to a single rotation of …. ….

2 Rotate the shape.

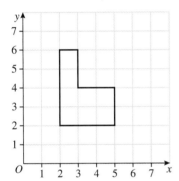

   a 90° clockwise about (0, 0).
      Label the image A.

   b 180° about (0, 0).
      Label the image B.

   c 90° anticlockwise about (0, 0).
      Label the image C.

3 Repeat question **2** for the shapes below.

   a 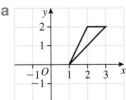   **b**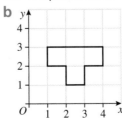

19.3 Exercise B

For each question copy the diagram then answer the question.

1

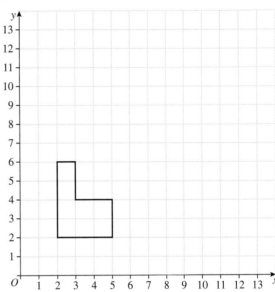

   a Rotate the shape 90 degrees clockwise about the point (6, 1). Label the image A.

   b Rotate the shape 180 degrees about the point (5, 6). Label the image B.

2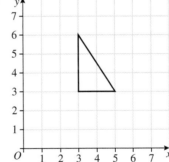

   a Rotate the triangle 90 degrees anticlockwise about the point (3, 3). Label the image A.

   b Rotate the triangle 180 degrees about the point (5, 3). Label the image B.

   c Write down the coordinates of the vertices of the images A and B.

3 The diagram shows two identical shapes
A and B.
Describe fully the single transformation
which takes
a shape A to shape B
b shape B to shape A.

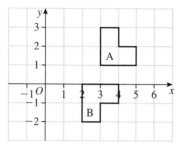

4

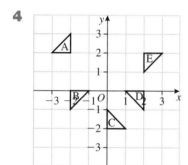

a Triangle C is rotated 180 degrees
about (1, −1).
Which triangle is the image of C under
this transformation?
b Triangle A is rotated 90 degrees
clockwise about the point (−3, −1).
Which triangle is the image of A under
this transformation?
c Describe fully the single transformation
which will take
  i B to A
  ii C to A
  iii D to A
  iv E to A

19.4 Exercise A

1 On a copy of the following diagram,
translate the shape
a 4 units to the right and 1 unit up
b 2 units to the right and 8 units down
c 4 units to the left and no units up
d 3 units to the left and 5 units down.

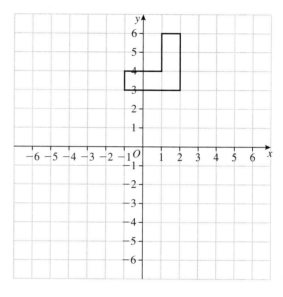

2 Describe the transformation which takes
shape A to
a shape B   **b** shape C
c shape D   **d** shape E

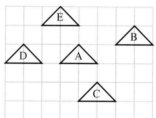

3 On squared paper draw and label x and
y-axes from −12 to 12
a Draw the rectangle with coordinates
A(−3, 8), B(4, 8), C(4, 5) and D(−3, 5)
b Draw the image of ABCD after a
translation 8 units to the right and 1
unit up.
Label this image G.
c Draw the image of ABCD after a
translation 4 units to the right and
10 units down.
Label this image H.
d Draw the image of ABCD after a
translation 5 units to the left and
14 units down.
Label this image I.
e Describe the transformation of
  i shape G to shape H
  ii shape G to shape I
  iii shape H to shape I

19.4 Exercise B

1 a Write the following translations as vectors
  i 3 units right and 7 units up
  ii 5 units right and 2 units down
  iii 11 units left and 8 units down
  iv 6 units left and 4 units up

b Describe in words the translations given by the following vectors

  i $\begin{pmatrix} -9 \\ 1 \end{pmatrix}$ **ii** $\begin{pmatrix} 5 \\ 6 \end{pmatrix}$ **iii** $\begin{pmatrix} 3 \\ -10 \end{pmatrix}$ **iv** $\begin{pmatrix} -7 \\ -6 \end{pmatrix}$

2 Use vectors to describe these translations

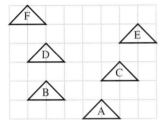

a	B to C	**b**	B to E
c	A to C	**d**	A to D
e	F to E	**f**	F to A
g	E to D	**h**	E to B
i	D to B	**j**	C to D

3 Draw a grid with the x- and y-axes from -7 to 7

a Plot and join the coordinates $(3, -1)$, $(5, -1)$, $(5, -3)$, $(6, -3)$, $(4, -5)$, $(2, -3)$ $(3, -3)$ and $(3, -1)$ to make an arrow shape.

b **i** Transform the arrow by a translation of $\begin{pmatrix} 1 \\ 8 \end{pmatrix}$, label the image A.

  ii Write down the vector which would translate image A back to the original arrow.

c **i** Transform the arrow by a translation of $\begin{pmatrix} -8 \\ 6 \end{pmatrix}$, label the image B.

  ii Write down the vector which would translate image B back to the original arrow.

d Describe the transformation from
  i shape A to shape B
  ii shape B to shape A.

Chapter 20

20.1 Exercise A

1 This graph can be used to convert between miles and kilometres.

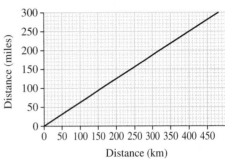

a Use the graph to convert
  i 250 miles to kilometres
  ii 150 miles to kilometres.

b Use the graph to convert
  i 50 kilometres to miles
  ii 220 kilometres to miles.

c Kieran drives 320 km from his home to London.
Stacy drives 220 miles from her home to London.
Kieran says that he drives further than Stacy. Is he correct? Show your working.

2 A bank sells euros (€) at the rate of €1.4 = £1

a Copy and complete the table.

British pounds (£)	0	10	20	100
Euros (€)	0			

b Copy the grid. Draw a graph to convert euros to pounds.

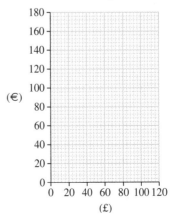

c **i** How many euros does Ian buy for
£60?

  ii How many euros does
Miss Simpson buy for £150?

  iii Leanne buys €56
How many British pounds is this?

  iv Mr Newton buys €420
How many British pounds is this?

20.1 Exercise B

1 A mobile phone bill is calculated from

fixed charge + charge for number of minutes used

The graph shows the bill for different numbers of minutes used.

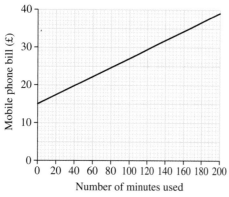

a Use the graph to find the bill when 150 minutes are used.

b Gina's bill was £24. How many minutes did she use?

c How much is the fixed charge?

d Work out the cost for one minute in pence.

20.2 Exercise A

1 The graph shows Bill's journey by bicycle to visit a friend.

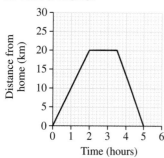

a How far is it from Bill's house to his friend's house?

b How long does Bill spend at his friend's house?

c How long does it take Bill to cycle home?

d What is the total number of hours Bill is away from home?

2 The distance–time graph shows a coach journey between Cardiff and Dorchester.

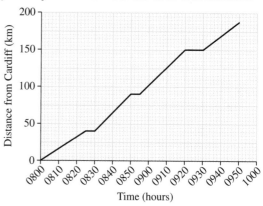

a What time does the coach leave Cardiff?

b How far is it from Cardiff to Dorchester?

c How many times does the coach stop on the journey?
Give a reason for your answer.

d For how long does the coach stop in total during the journey?

e How long does the coach take to travel from Cardiff to Dorchester?

20.2 Exercise B

1 A car travels from Middlesbrough to Aberdeen, a distance of 280 miles, at an average speed of 56 miles per hour. The distance–time graph shows the journey.

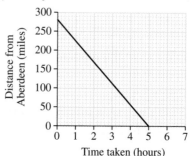

a A bus leaves Aberdeen at the same time as the car leaves Middlesbrough. The bus travels on the same route and takes 7 hours to get to Middlesbrough.
Work out the average speed of the bus.

b   **i** Copy the graph. On the same grid draw the distance–time graph for the bus.

ii Clearly mark on the graph the point at which the car and the bus pass each other.

iii At what distance from Aberdeen does the car pass the bus?

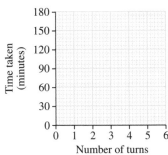

20.3 Exercise A

1 The London Eye makes one complete turn every 30 minutes.

a Copy and complete the table.

Number of turns	0	1	2	3	4	5	6
Number of minutes							

b On a copy of the grid, draw a graph to show the information given in the table.

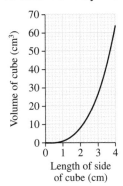

c How many turns does the London Eye make in 75 minutes?

d How long does it take the London Eye to make $4\frac{1}{2}$ turns?

2 Jamie knows that 1 ounce is 25 g.

a Use this information to draw a conversion graph on a copy of the following grid.

b Use the graph to convert
  i 180 g to ounces
  ii 2.4 ounces to grams.

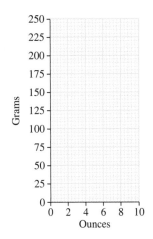

c A recipe needs 130 g of flour. Harry has 4.8 ounces of flour. Does Harry have enough flour for the recipe?
Show your working.

20.3 Exercise B

1 The graph shows the volume of cubes up to size 4 cm by 4 cm by 4 cm.

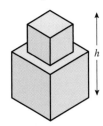

a Use the graph to find the volume of a cube of side 3 cm.

b Two cubes are placed together, one on top of the other to form a tower.

The total volume of the two cubes is 72 cm³. The sides of each cube are a whole number of centimetres.
Use the graph to help work out the height, h, of the tower.

2 Graham records the temperature in his garden every two hours one day. The graph shows his results.

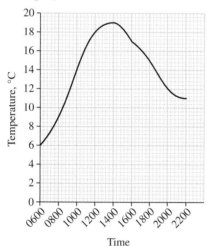

a What was the temperature at 0800?

b What was the maximum temperature Graham recorded?

c By how many degrees did the temperature fall between 1800 and 2200?

d What was the minimum recorded temperature?

e Over which two hour period did the temperature increase the most?

Chapter 21

21.1 Exercise A

1 There were 120 visitors to a children's farm one Saturday.
The number of men, women and children is shown in the table.

	Number	Angle
Men	20	
Women	35	
Children	65	

a Copy and complete the table.

b Draw a pie chart to represent this information.

2 The 72 employees in a company were asked how they usually travel to work.

The table shows their replies.

Car	32
Train	21
Bus	11
Cycle	5
Walk	3
Total	**72**

Draw a pie chart to represent this information.

3 The table shows the number of each type of housing being built on a new estate.

Apartments	50
Terraced houses	72
Semi-detached houses	84
Detached houses	34
Total	**240**

Draw a pie chart to represent this data.

21.1 Exercise B

1 The pie chart shows the favourite sports of a group of students.

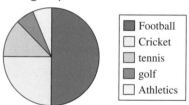

a Which is the modal favourite sport?

b 160 students were asked in total. How many chose

  i cricket   ii tennis

  as their favourite sport?

2 The Alpha Car Hire company hired out 180 cars one week.
The pie chart shows the number of cars hired each day.

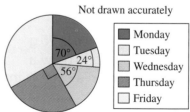

a What fraction of the total number of people hired a car on Thursday?

b How many people hired a car on Monday or Tuesday?

c **i** Calculate the angle for Friday.

ii How many people hired a car on Friday?

21.2 Exercise A

1 The number of empty seats on a bus was recorded each hour from 7 am to 9 pm. The results were

23 7 14 2 34 19 23 10
37 5 7 21 19 16 25

a Draw an ordered stem and leaf diagram to represent this data. Include a key.

b Use the diagram to work out the median.

c Write down the range of the number of empty seats.

2 The number of visitors to a museum were recorded each day for two weeks. These are the results:

123 156 133 110 117 141 138
129 120 144 107 135 138 121

a Copy and complete the stem and leaf diagram.

Key .... | ..... represents ....

```
10 |
11 |
12 |
13 |
14 |
15 |
```

b On how many days were there more than 140 visitors?

c Write down the mode.

3 Adam works in an office. He records the number of letters he posts each day for three weeks.

35 43 41 52 28 50 32 43 17
48 22 26 36 39 36

Adam attempts to draw an ordered stem and leaf diagram to show these amounts.

This is his diagram.

Key 2 | 3 represents 32 letters

```
1 | 7
2 | 2 8 6
3 | 2 5 6 6 9
4 | 1 3 8
5 | 0 2
```

Adam has made three mistakes. Describe the mistakes he has made.

21.2 Exercise B

1 The stem and leaf diagram shows the number of texts sent by 15 teenagers one day.

Key 1 | 2 represents 12 texts

```
0 | 4 5 9
1 | 2 3 6 8
2 | 0 5 6 7 9
3 | 1 3 8
```

a How many teenagers sent less than 10 texts?

b What was the greatest number of texts sent?

c Work out the median number of texts sent.

d Work out the range.

2 The stem and leaf diagram shows the number of rooms booked in a hotel each night for 14 nights.

Key 4 | 1 represents 41 rooms

```
4 | 1 9
5 | 2 5 6 6 8
6 | 4 7 8 9
7 | 2 3 5
```

a Work out the range.

b Write down the modal number of rooms booked.

c Calculate the median number of rooms booked.

d On the 15th night there were 70 rooms booked.

If this number was added to the stem and leaf diagram describe what effect it would have on

i the range   **ii** the median.

21.3 Exercise A

1 The shoe sizes and heights of seven teenagers are shown in the table.

Shoe size	2	3	4.5	5	6	6.5	7
Height (cm)	140	146	152	154	160	163	168

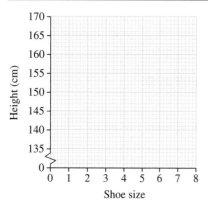

a Plot the data as a scatter graph.
b Describe the relationship shown by the graph.
c Draw a line of best fit.
d Use your line of best fit to estimate the height of a teenager with shoe size 4

2 Seven pupils were asked how much time each of them spent watching TV and each of them spent doing homework one evening.
Their results are shown in the table.

Time spent watching TV (mins)	30	40	45	60	90	120	150
Time spent doing homework (mins)	125	120	100	110	80	60	35

a Plot the data as a scatter diagram.
b Write down the type of correlation shown by the scatter diagram.
c Draw a line of best fit.
d Another pupil spent 45 minutes doing homework.
Use your line of best fit to estimate the number of minutes this pupil spent watching TV.

21.3 Exercise B

1 a Write down the strength and type of correlation shown in each of the scatter graphs below.

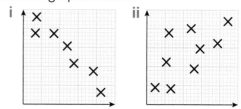

b The marks for a group of pupils who sat two tests are shown in the scatter graph.

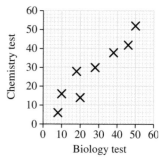

 i Draw a line of best fit on a copy of the graph.
 ii Use your line of best fit to estimate the biology test mark for a pupil who scored 20 marks in the chemistry test.

2 The table shows the number of hours of sunshine and the maximum temperature at six seaside resorts one day.

Hours of sunshine	6	7.5	9	10	10	11
Maximum temperature (°C)	18	20	21	24	25	28

a Plot a scatter graph for this data.
b Draw a line of best fit on your scatter graph.
c Describe the strength and type of correlation shown by the graph.
d Use your line of best fit to estimate the temperature at a seaside resort which had 8 hours of sunshine.
e Explain why the line of best fit should not be used to estimate the temperature at a seaside resort which had 15 hours of sunshine.

21.4 Exercise A

1 Chris delivers pizza each evening from Tuesday to Saturday.
The time series graph shows the number of deliveries he has each night for two weeks.

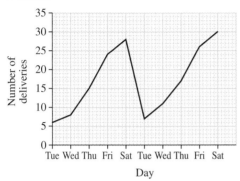

a Describe a pattern in the data.
b How many deliveries were made on Friday of the first week?
c Calculate the range of the number of deliveries.

2 The table shows the average monthly rainfall for England and Scotland for the first six months of 2006

	January	February	March	April	May	June
England	35	56	94	46	112	25
Scotland	109	85	137	106	112	73

Average monthly rainfall (mm)

a Draw time series graphs for the two countries on the same axes.
b Which country is generally wetter throughout the first six months of the year?
Give a reason for your answer.
c Which country has the greater range of average monthly rainfall?
Show your working.

21.4 Exercise B

1 Each month a puppy is weighed.
The following graph shows its weight each month from 3 months to 6 months.
At 7 months the puppy weighed 3.9 kg and at 10 months it weighed 4.4 kg.

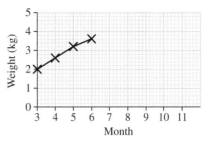

a Copy and complete the graph.
Join the points with straight lines.
b Use the graph to estimate the weight of the puppy
  i at 8 months
  ii at 11 months.
c Explain why it would not be sensible to use the graph to estimate the weight of the puppy at 18 months.

Chapter 22

22.1 Exercise A

1 Write down the values of each of the following
  a 6^2 **b** 8^2 **c** 5^2 **d** 3^2
  e 15^2 **f** 40^2 **g** 70^2

2 Work out the values of each of the following
  a $7^2 + 4^2$ **b** $11^2 + 8^2$
  c $13^2 - 5^2$ **d** $9^2 - 6^2$

3 Work out the values of each of the following
  a 30^3 **b** 400^3 **c** 2000^3

4 Use the square numbers up to 144 to work out
  a 0.3^2 **b** 0.5^2
  c 0.8^2 **d** 1.2^2

5 Work out the values of each of the following using positive square roots
  a $7^2 + \sqrt{169}$ **b** $\sqrt{121} + 3^3$
  c $\sqrt{196} - \sqrt{64}$ **d** $5^3 - \sqrt{81}$
  e $\sqrt{25} + \sqrt{49}$ **f** $15^2 - \sqrt{100}$

22.1 Exercise B

1 Write down the square numbers from the list

64 20 130 169 25 60 225 120 144

2 $\sqrt{2209} = 47$
Write down the values of
a $\sqrt{220\,900}$ b $\sqrt{22.09}$ c 0.47^2

3 Explain how you know that 125 is **not** a square number.

4 Use a calculator to find the two integers between which $\sqrt{560}$ lies.

5 Use a calculator to find the smallest square number that is greater than 2500

6 Use a calculator to find the two integers between which $\sqrt[3]{400}$ lies.

22.2 Exercise A

1 Round the following numbers to one significant figure
a 32   b 78   c 15   d 246
e 708   f 372   g 2300   h 9009
i 6870   j 4295

2 Round the following decimals to one significant figure
a 3.46   b 1.72   c 0.56   d 0.89
e 12.34   f 0.076   g 9.9   h 0.62
i 5.54   j 37.26

3 Kieran spends £17 correct to the nearest pound.
What are the maximum and minimum amounts that Kieran could have spent?

22.2 Exercise B

1 The following quantities are given to the nearest whole number.
Write down the lower and upper bounds for each quantity.
a 20 kg   b 45 m
c 8 miles   d 72 grams
e 100 litres   f 6 gallons

2 The following measures are each given to one significant figure.
Write down the lower and upper bounds for each number.
a 5 minutes   b 70 cm
c 0.4 kg   d 0.08 m

3 The distance from Bristol to Redcar is 250 miles to the nearest 5 miles.
Rob drives from Bristol to Redcar and back again.
What is the shortest distance his journey could be?

22.3 Exercise A

1 Use approximations to estimate the value of each of the following.
a $\dfrac{3.9 \times 5.1}{1.8}$ b $\dfrac{7.8 \times 5.9}{4.2}$
c $\dfrac{6.2 \times 8.9}{5.9}$ d $\dfrac{8.3 \times 3.2}{2.2}$
e $\dfrac{39.3 \times 5.8}{19.7}$ f $\dfrac{4.1 \times 10.23}{5.2}$

2 Use approximations to estimate the value of each of the following.
a $\dfrac{103.6 \times 4.1}{1.1 + 2.8}$ b $\dfrac{198 \times 6.3}{5.7 + 6.1}$
c $\dfrac{985 \times 2.9}{2.2 + 0.9}$

3 Estimate the cost of
a 30 pens at 49p each
b eight drinks at 99p each
c 3.1 metres of ribbon at 29p per metre
d nine books at £4.99 each
e 52 litres of fuel at 97p per litre

4 Use the formula
$$\text{Average speed} = \frac{\text{Distance}}{\text{Time}}$$
to estimate the average speed for each of the following journeys.
a 198 miles in 4 hours and 5 minutes
b 32 km in 2.9 hours
c 6300 miles in 9 hours 57 minutes.

22.3 Exercise B

1 Use approximations to estimate the value of each of the following.

a $\dfrac{7.9}{0.41}$ b $\dfrac{9.83}{0.48}$

c $\dfrac{20.3}{0.51}$ d $\dfrac{39.4}{0.2}$

2 Use approximations to estimate the value of each of the following.

a $\dfrac{7.1 \times 3.8}{0.41}$ b $\dfrac{6.05 \times 5.01}{0.29}$

c $\dfrac{20.4 \times 4.8}{0.19}$ d $\dfrac{8.12 \times 2.07}{0.39}$

3 Which is smaller

$6 \div 0.32$, $5 \div 0.2$ or $9 \div 0.3$

4 Abdul says that $73 \times 6.2 = 4526$
Use estimation to show that he is **not** correct.

5 a Estimate the value of $\dfrac{5.97}{0.29}$ by rounding each number to one significant figure.

b Work out the difference between the estimated value of $\dfrac{5.97}{0.29}$ and the exact value.

22.4 Exercise A

1 Write down the reciprocal of the following numbers.
Leave your answer as a fraction.

a 7 b 15
c 22 d −17
e −50

2 Work out the reciprocal of the following integers.
Give your answer **i** as a fraction
ii as a decimal.

a 6 b 9
c 10 d 100
e 1000

3 Write down the reciprocal of the following fractions.
Leave your answer as an improper fraction.

a $\frac{3}{7}$ b $\frac{5}{8}$ c $\frac{4}{11}$ d $\frac{3}{5}$ e $\frac{2}{9}$

4 Use a calculator to work out the reciprocal of the following decimals. Where necessary give your answer as a decimal to two decimal places.

a 0.1 b 0.125 c 1.4
d 5.5 e 3.1

5 Match the pairs of reciprocals.

22.4 Exercise B

1 Use reciprocals to work out these divisions.

a $6 \div 10$ b $4 \div \frac{1}{2}$
c $\frac{1}{4} \div \frac{3}{8}$ d $\frac{2}{5} \div 8$

2 Which is greater, the reciprocal of 6 or the reciprocal of 4?
Explain your answer.

3 Add together the reciprocal of 5 and the reciprocal of 4
Give your answer as a decimal.

4 Multiply together the reciprocal of 8 and the reciprocal of 10
Give your answer as a decimal.

Chapter 23

23.1 Exercise A

1 Copy and complete these sentences.

a The three figure bearing for west is ....

b The three figure bearing for south-east is ....

c The three figure bearing for north is ....

2 Copy and complete these statements using the words North, South, East or West.

   a A bearing of 110° is between .... and ....

   b A bearing of 40° is between .... and ....

   c A bearing of 225° is between .... and ....

   d A bearing of 350° is between .... and ....

3 Use a protractor to draw accurate diagrams to represent these bearings.

   a 065°   **b** 080°   **c** 115°   **d** 162°

   e 190°   **f** 226°   **g** 285°   **h** 318°

4 Reanne is walking north-east and turns through half a turn. Which direction is she now facing?

23.1 Exercise B

1 The map shows the position of two boats *A* and *B* and a lighthouse *L*.

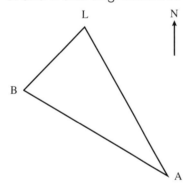

   a Measure the bearing of boat *A* from the lighthouse *L*.

   b Measure the bearing of boat *B* from the lighthouse *L*.

   c Measure the bearing of boat *A* from boat *B*.

   d What is the bearing of boat *B* from boat *A*?

2 Rainton is on a bearing of 132° from Sigbeck.

   What is the bearing of Sigbeck from Rainton? Use a sketch to help you.

3 This is a map of a village.

   A, *B* and *C* are houses in the village.

   P is the post office and *S* is the school.

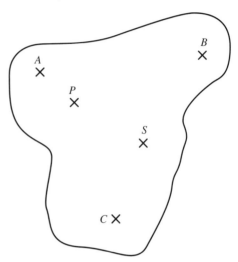

   a Which house is on a bearing of 160° from the post office, *P*?

   b Which house is on a bearing of 35° from the school, *S*?

   c Measure and write down the bearing of the school, *S* from the post office, *P*.

23.2 Exercise A

 1 Models are made using a scale of 1 cm to represent 4 m.

   a A model boat is 5 cm long. What is the length of the real boat?

   b A model house is 2.5 cm high. What is the height of the real house?

2 Here is a plan of a house. Use a scale of 1 cm to 2 m to make an accurate scale drawing of the house.

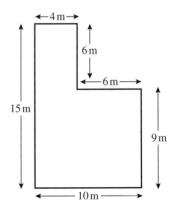

3 A map of a theme park has a scale of 1 cm : 50 m.

  a The Big Dipper ride and the Haunted House are 425 m apart.
How far apart are they on the map?

  b The cafe and the Bumper Cars are 6.2 cm apart on the map.
What is the actual distance from the cafe to the Bumper Cars?

4 A map has a scale of 1 : 50 000
Two towns are 4 cm apart on the map.
Find the actual distance, in kilometres, between the two towns.

23.2 Exercise B

1 Here is a sketch of a triangle. Use a scale of 1 cm : 100 mm to make an accurate scale drawing of the triangle.

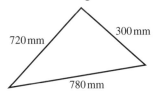

2 A lighthouse, *L*, is on the coast. A ship, *S*, is 4 kilometres due west of *L*.
Another ship, *T*, is 7 kilometres due south of *L*.

  a Make an accurate scale drawing to show the positions of *L*, *S* and *T*.
Use a scale of 2 cm to 1 km.

  b Use your scale drawing to work out the distance of ship *S* from ship *T*.

3 The diagram shows the positions of *A* and *B*.
The diagram is drawn to a scale of 1 cm to represent 5 km.

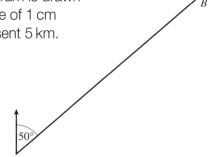

  a What is the bearing of *A* from *B*?

  b Use the diagram to calculate the actual distance of *B* from *A*.

  c *C* is due South of *A* and on a bearing of 195° from *B*.
Mark the position of *C* on a copy of the diagram.

Chapter 24

24.1 Exercise A

1 The two-way table shows the year group and gender of the members of a school gymnastics club.

	Y7	**Y8**	**Y9**
Male	12	8	11
Female	17	20	15

  a How many members of the gym club are in Y8?

  b How many of the members of the gym club are male?

  c Work out the total number of members in the gym club.

2 The 150 employees in a company were asked how they usually travel to work.
The two-way table shows the method of travel and gender of the employees.
One of the entries is missing.

	Car	**Bus**	**Train**	**Walk**
Male	47	9	19	3
Female	41		14	5

  a Copy and complete the table.

  b How many of the employees are female?

  c How many employees travel to work by train?

  d How many employees do **not** travel to work by car?

3 The incomplete two-way table shows the activities chosen by adults and children at a leisure centre one afternoon.

	Swimming	Football	Badminton	Ice-skating
Adults		20	9	14
Children	26	10		

a Copy the table. Use the following information to complete it.
  ● No children played badminton.
  ● There were three times as many children as adults taking part in ice-skating.
  ● 57 people went swimming.

b Calculate the total number of
  i adults   ii children.

c For which activity were there twice as many adults as children?

24.1 Exercise B

1 100 men, 100 women and 100 children were asked if they are left-handed, right-handed or ambidextrous (able to use both hands equally).
The results are shown in the chart.

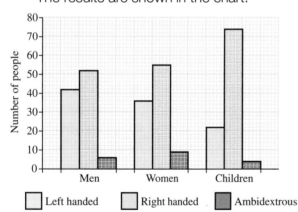

a Design and complete a two-way table for the results.

b Calculate the total number of people from this sample of 300 who are
  i left-handed   ii right-handed
  iii ambidextrous

2 Of 500 visitors to a London museum one weekend, 30% of the English visitors and 40% of the foreign visitors were male.
Three fifths of the visitors were English.

a Design and complete a two-way table for the data.

b Use your two-way table to work out the total number of female visitors.

24.2 Exercise A

1 The number of goals scored by a hockey team in their first 20 matches of the season are shown in the table.

Number of goals (x)	Frequency (f)	fx
0	4	
1	5	
2	8	
3	3	

a Copy and complete the table.

b Work out the mean number of goals per match.

2 The number of children in 50 families is shown in the table.

Number of children (x)	Frequency (f)	fx
0	5	
1	9	
2	18	
3	13	
4	4	
5	1	

Calculate the mean number of children per family.

3 A spinner has scores 1, 2, 3, 4 and 5 on its sides. The spinner is spun 30 times. The table shows the results.

Spinner score	Frequency
1	7
2	5
3	4
4	6
5	8

Calculate the mean score for this spinner.

24.2 Exercise B

1 a

Number	Frequency
2	8
3	6
4	4
5	2

Find the mean of this frequency distribution.

b If every number is increased by one but the frequencies stay the same, what would the new mean be?

c Look at this frequency distribution.

Number	Frequency
4	8
6	6
8	4
10	2

i Predict the mean of this distribution.

ii Check your prediction by calculating the mean.

2 The number of tomatoes on 25 plants are counted.
The table shows the results.

Number of tomatoes	Frequency
6	2
7	3
8	7
9	x
10	5

a Find the value of x.

b Find the mean number of tomatoes per plant.

3 The following table shows information about the number of children absent from a class each day.

Number absent	Frequency
1	7
3	4
x	5
6	3
7	1

a Work out Σf and an expression for Σfx.

b The mean number of children absent
= 3.2
Use your answers to part **a** to show that $x = 4$

24.3 Exercise A

1 Some male athletes were asked to record their best time for completing the 400 m sprint.
Their results are shown below.
Some female athletes were asked for the same information.
Their results are also shown below.

Male athletes

Range of times	12 seconds
Mean of times	56 seconds

Female athletes

Range of times	8 seconds
Mean of times	67 seconds

Compare the range and the mean of the two sets of times.

2 The number of goals scored by a school netball 'A' team in 10 matches is shown below.

7 8 3 6 11 5 4 9 7 6

a Write down the range.

b Calculate the mean.

The same data is collected for the netball 'B' team. The results have a range of 4 and a mean of 5.1
Compare the results of the two teams.

24.3 Exercise B

1   The two stem and leaf diagrams show the number of students in each session in 20 karate classes and 20 judo classes at a sports centre.

Karate   Key 1│8 represents 18 students

```
1│3 3 7 8
2│0 0 0 1 1 3 5 8 9
3│0 2 2 4 5 6 8
```

Judo   Key 0│6 represents 6 students

```
0│4 4 5 6 6 7 9 9
1│0 1 2 2 2 4 4 5 9
2│0 0 1
```

Compare the two stem and leaf diagrams.

2   The table shows information about the number of times the phone rang in a doctor's surgery per hour over 20 one-hour periods.

Number of times phone rang	Frequency
13	4
15	6
16	7
18	3

a   Write down the range.
b   Calculate the mean number of calls per hour.
c   The following month the surgery introduced appointment booking by internet.
    The number of times the phone rang per hour was again recorded and gave a range of 7 and a mean of 13.2
    Did the introduction of internet booking reduce the number of phone calls to the surgery?
    Explain your answer.

3   The following bar charts show the number of hours of sunshine each day in May in two coastal resorts, one on the East coast and one on the West coast.

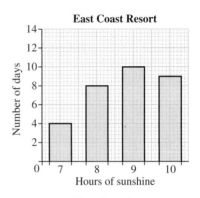

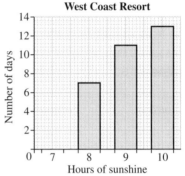

Compare the two distributions.

Chapter 25

25.1 Exercise A

1   Copy and complete
    a $\frac{7}{10} = \frac{}{100} = \ldots\ldots\%$
    b $\frac{6}{25} = \frac{}{100} = \ldots\ldots\%$
    c $\frac{1}{4} = \frac{}{100} = \ldots\ldots\%$
    d $\frac{3}{5} = \frac{}{100} = \ldots\ldots\%$

2   a   Write 4 as a percentage of 10
    b   Write 1 as a percentage of 5
    c   Write 75 as a percentage of 150
    d   Write 6 as a percentage of 20

3   a   Write 3 cm as a percentage of 8 cm.
    b   Write 4 kg as a percentage of 16 kg.
    c   Write 20 cm as a percentage of 1 metre.
    d   Write 60p as a percentage of £1

4   In each part leave your answer to one decimal place.
    a   Write 2 as a percentage of 3
    b   Write 7 as a percentage of 9

c Write 2 cm as a percentage of 6 cm.

d Write 50 cl as a percentage of 60 cl.

5 In a school of 1500 students, 845 are boys.
What percentage are boys?
Write your answer to one decimal place.

6 A small aircraft holds 150 litres of fuel when full.
130 litres of fuel are in the tank.
What percentage is this?

25.1 Exercise B

1 In a class of 30 students, 21 are girls.
What percentage of the students are boys?

2 A bag contains 14 blue pencils, 13 red pencils and 3 purple pencils.
What percentage of the pencils are **not** purple?

3 Darren, Matt, Shaun, Tom and Trevor form a five a side football team.
What percentage of the players' names do **not** start with the letter T?

4 In a survey 13 out of 20 girls have fair hair and 11 out of 25 boys have fair hair.
What percentage of the whole survey has fair hair?
Write your answer to one decimal place.

5 At a dog kennel there are 75 dogs.
16 of these dogs are pedigrees.
What percentage are pedigrees? Write your answer to one decimal place.

6 In a mathematics test a student scores 34 out of 75
In a science test the same student scores 11 out of 25
In which test did the student do better?
Explain your answer by giving the percentage mark for each test.

25.2 Exercise A

1 Increase each of the following quantities by 10%
  a 500 fish   **b** 90 grams
  c 60 m   **d** 50 miles

2 Decrease each of the following quantities by 25%
  a 1200 people   **b** 40 pence
  c 20 kg   **d** 120 minutes

3 Increase each of the following quantities by 5%
  a 40 people   **b** 80 buttons
  c 30 cm   **d** 180°

4 Decrease each of the following quantities by 20%
  a 200 tonne   **b** 70 litres
  c £2.20   **d** 90°

5 **a** Increase 42 kg by 25%
   b Decrease 90 grams by 30%

6 Write down the multiplier for each of the following percentage increases.
  a 14%   **b** 7%   **c** 50%

7 Write down the multiplier for each of the following percentage decreases.
  a 22%   **b** 6%   **c** 10%

8 Use the multiplier method to
  a increase 1250 km by 42%
  b increase 260 litres by 82%
  c decrease 24 hours by 32%
  d decrease £64 by 7%

25.2 Exercise B

1 Edna receives an electricity bill for £160
VAT is added at 5%
How much is the total bill?

2 Mr Cadman sees a television set advertised for £800
A discount of 15% is given.
How much does he pay?

3 A salesperson sells three windows for £900
She receives commission of 20% of the selling price.
How much commission does she receive?

4 The number of students in a school was 1350 last year.
This increased by 8%
How many students are there now?

5 Referees in a league gave out 12% more yellow and red cards this season than last season.
Last season they gave out 2800 cards.
How many more cards did they give out this season?

6 The population of Russia was 145.5 million last year. This year the population has fallen by 0.5%
What is the population this year?

25.3 Exercise A

1 Work out the percentage change for each of the following.
   a Increasing 36 by 9
   b Decreasing 60 by 12
   c Increasing 25 by 25
   d Decreasing 50 by 40

2 Work out the percentage change for each of the following.
   a Increasing from 50 to 60
   b Decreasing from 32 to 24
   c Increasing from 48 miles to 60 miles
   d Decreasing from 60 cm to 54 cm

3 Work out the percentage change for each of the following.
   a Increasing 320 miles by 64 miles
   b Decreasing 500 minutes by 75 minutes
   c Increasing from 95 litres to 380 litres
   d Decreasing from 920 kg to 900 kg

4 Which of the following statements represent a 25% change?
   a 40 changes to 30
   b 40 changes to 50
   c 40 changes to 65

25.3 Exercise B

1 A car is bought for £8000 then sold for £6000
Find the percentage loss.

2 The number of sheep on a farm increases from 200 to 300
Work out the percentage increase.

3 The cost of a projector falls from £1200 to £900
Work out the percentage fall.

4 The value of an antique increases from £2400 to £2900
Calculate the percentage increase.

5 An insurance company reduces its workforce from 17 500 to 13 500
Calculate the percentage reduction.

6 Which is the greater percentage change, increasing from 120 to 160 or decreasing from 160 to 120?
Explain your answer.

25.4 Exercise A

1 Work out the simple interest on each of the following for
   i 1 year
   ii 3 years
   iii 5 years.
   a £5000 at 10% per year
   b £600 at 5% per year.

2 Work out the value of the following investments after
   i 1 year
   ii 2 years.
   a £200 at 10% per year
   b £800 at 3% per year

3 Rupert invested £200 at 4% simple interest.
He received £32 interest in total. For how many years did he invest?

4 For each of the following loans work out
 i the simple interest using the formula
 $$I = \frac{PRT}{100}$$
 ii the total amount repaid.
 a £15 000 at 5% per year for 2 years
 b £4800 at 4.2% per year for 3 years

5 Belinda lends £3600 to her son.
He agrees to pay back 5% of the initial loan every 6 months.
How long does it take him to pay off the loan?

6 A loan of £4200 for 4 years has simple interest added of £1344
Work out the interest rate.

25.4 Exercise B

1 The annual rate of inflation is 2%
Use the annual rate of inflation to work out the prices after one year of
 a a TV costing £800 this year
 b a bicycle costing £120 this year
 c a shed costing £70 this year.

2 Mr Paye earns £15 000 per year.
He pays income tax at the rate of 20%
How much tax does he pay?

3 Bill earns £17 500 per year.
The first £4500 is tax free.
He pays income tax at the rate of 25%
How much tax does he pay?

4 The annual rate of inflation is 8%
Use the annual rate of inflation to work out the prices after one year of
 a a cottage costing £166 000 this year
 b a van costing £7400 this year
 c a bed costing £360 this year.

5 The first £5200 of earnings is tax free.
Income tax is paid at the rate of 10% on the next £6000
Income tax is paid at the rate of 22% on the remainder.
 a Mrs Pound earns £38 000 per year.
 How much tax does she pay?
 b Miss Penny earns £20 000
 How much tax does she pay?

Chapter 26

26.1 Exercise A

1 Write each of the following in index form
 a $6 \times 6 \times 6 \times 6 \times 6$
 b $8 \times 8 \times 8 \times 8 \times 8 \times 8 \times 8$
 c $2 \times 2 \times 7 \times 7 \times 7 \times 7$
 d $5 \times 5 \times 5 \times 5 \times 9 \times 9 \times 9 \times 9 \times 9 \times 9$

2 Write each of the following in index form.
 a $x \times x \times x \times x \times x$
 b $y \times y \times y \times y \times y \times y \times y$
 c $a \times a \times a \times b \times b \times b$
 d $p \times p \times p \times p \times p \times p \times q \times q$

3 Write each of the following using multiplication symbols.
 a 5^2 **b** 2^7
 c $2^3 \times 4^2$ **d** $3^2 \times 4 \times 5^4$

4 Write each of the following using multiplication symbols.
 a x^4 **b** $p^3 q r^2$

5 Use your knowledge of squares and cubes to work out the value of each letter symbol in the following.
 a $2^a = 8$ **b** $3^b = 9$
 c $10^c = 100$

 6 You are given that $A = x^3 + y^4$ and $B = x^3 y^4$.
Find the values of A and B when
 a $x = 3$ and $y = 5$
 b $x = 6$ and $y = 9$

7 The letter symbols in the following expressions represent positive integers. Use the power button on a scientific calculator to find their values.

a $6^a = 7776$ b $8^b = 2\,097\,152$

26.1 Exercise B

1 Find the value of the letter symbol in each of the following.

a $2^a = 2^3 \times 2^4$ b $3^b = 3^5 \times 3^8$
c $5^c = 5^7 \div 5^3$ d $7^d = 7^6 \times 7^2 \div 7^4$

2 Simplify each of the following.

a $x^4 \times x^2$ b $y^3 \times y$
c $t^6 \div t^2$ d $s^9 \div s^8$
e $p^3 \times p^5 \div p$ f $\dfrac{(q^2 \times q^4)}{(q \times q^3)}$

3 Simplify each of the following.

a $2x^3 \times 3x^2$ b $4y \times 2y^3$
c $12t^5 \div 4t^3$ d $18s^{10} \div 9s^5$

4 a Copy and complete this table of powers of 5

5^1	5^2	5^3	5^4	5^5	5^6
5					

Use the table to work out

b 25^2 c $15\,625 \div 125$

26.2 Exercise A

1 Copy and complete the grids.

a $4(x + 6)$

×	x	6
4	$4 \times x =$	$4 \times 6 =$	$4x + 24$

b $5(3x - 7)$

×	$3x$	-7
5		

c $-2(2x - 4y)$

×		
-2		

2 Expand each of these expressions.

a $3(a + 5)$ b $6(b + 1)$
c $4(c - 3)$ d $5(5 - d)$
e $-3(e + 4)$ f $7(x + y - 2)$

3 Expand each of these expressions.

a $4(2a + 7)$ b $2(3b + 4)$
c $5(2c - 1)$ d $8(2 - 3d)$
e $-2(6e + 5)$ f $4(3x - 2y + 1)$

4 Multiply out the brackets and simplify each of the following expressions.

a $2(3a + 7) + 4$ b $5(b - 6) - 1$
c $7(2c - 3) + 25$ d $3(1 - 2d) + d$
e $-2(e + 7) + 5e$
f $3(6x - y + 5) - 18x + 3y$

5 Chris expands $5(2x - 6)$. His answer is $7x - 11$. Explain what Chris has done wrong.

6 Work out

a $7 \times 40 + 7 \times 9$ b $7 \times (40 + 9)$
c What do you notice?

26.2 Exercise B

1 Expand each of these expressions.

a $a(a + 3)$ b $b(b - 4)$
c $c(c - 6)$ d $d(2 - d)$
e $e(3e + 4)$ f $x(x - 3y + 5)$

2 Expand each of these expressions.

a $3a(2a + 3)$ b $5b(3b - 2)$
c $3c^2(2c + 4)$ d $2d^2(1 - d)$
e $e^3(7e - 6)$ f $3xy(4x - y + 7)$

3 Multiply out the brackets and simplify each of the following expressions.

a $2(a + 4) + 6(a + 5)$
b $3(b + 1) + 6(b + 7)$
c $5(2c - 1) + 4(2c + 1)$
d $d(3d + 4) - 2d(d + 2)$
e $2e^2(3e - 2) - 3(4e^2 + 1)$
f $xy(x - y) + x(y^2 - 2)$

4 Show that $4(3x + 7) + 3(x + 4) = 5(3x + 8)$

5 Expand and simplify

a $(x + 2)(x + 3)$ b $(x + 5)(x - 2)$
c $(x - 6)(x + 4)$ d $(x - 1)(x - 1)$

6 Jack says that $3x^2(5x^4 + 2y) = 15x^8 + 6x^2y$. Explain why he is **not** correct.

26.3 Exercise A

1 a Copy and complete the following to find the factors of 15 and $10x$.

1×15	$3 \times \ldots$	$5 \times \ldots$	
$1 \times 10x$	$2 \times 5x$	$5 \times \ldots$	$10 \times \ldots$

b What is the highest common factor of 15 and $10x$?

c Factorise $15 + 10x$.

2 a Write a list of the factors of
  i $6a$ **ii** $8b$

b Factorise $6a + 8b$.

3 Copy and complete
  a $4a + 8 = 4(a + \ldots)$
  b $15b - 12 = 3(5b - \ldots)$
  c $6x - 4y = 2(\ldots - \ldots)$
  d $16x + 12y = \ldots (\ldots + \ldots)$

4 Factorise completely
  a $24x + 16y$ **b** $33x - 22y$
  c $50x - 75y$ **d** $36x + 48y$
  e $32x - 72y$ **f** $90x + 135y$

26.3 Exercise B

1 Lucy is asked to factorise completely
$5x^2 - 15x$
She gives the answer $5(x^2 - 3x)$.
Explain why she is wrong.

2 Copy and complete the diagram to show the factors of $8x^3 + 2x$

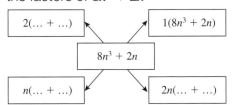

3 Copy and complete
  a $a^2 + 3a = a(a + \ldots)$
  b $b^2 - 4b = b(\ldots - \ldots)$
  c $5c^2 - 15c = 5c(\ldots - \ldots)$
  d $6x^3 + 12xy = 6x(\ldots + \ldots)$

4 Factorise completely
  a $a^2 + 5a$
  b $3b^2 - 4b$
  c $ax + bx + cx$
  d $8y^2 + 12y$
  e $5x + 15y - 20z$
  f $18x^4 + 24x^3 - 12x^2$

5 You are given that
$5(3x + 7) + 4(3x - 2) = a(x + b)$
Find the values of a and b.

Chapter 27

27.1 Exercise A

In the following exercises the diagrams are not drawn accurately.

 1 Write down the value of angle x in each of these diagrams.

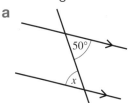
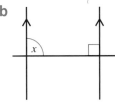

2 Write down the value of angle y in each of these diagrams.

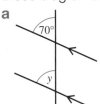
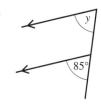

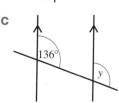

3 Work out the value of angle x in each of these diagrams.

a

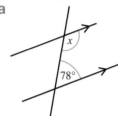

b

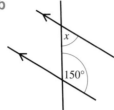

c

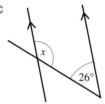

4 Work out the value of each angle marked by letters.
Give reasons for your answers.

a

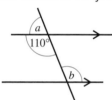

b

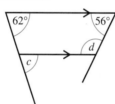

c

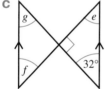

27.1 Exercise B

In the following exercise the diagrams are not drawn accurately.

 1 In each part, work out the values of the angles marked by letters.

a

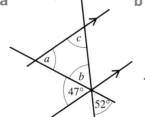

b

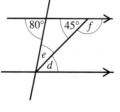

c

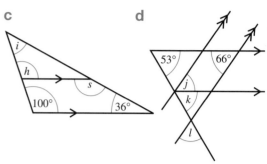

d

2 Look at these diagrams and answer the following questions. Give reasons for your answers.

a Are *AB* and *CD* parallel?

b Are *PQ* and *RS* parallel?

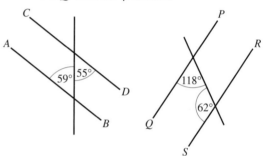

27.2 Exercise A

In the following exercise the diagrams are not drawn accurately.

1 Calculate the size of the angles marked by letters.

a

b

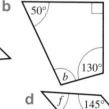

c

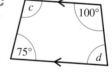

d

e

f

g

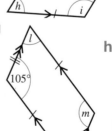

h

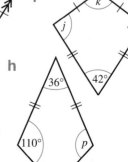

27.2 Exercise B

In the following exercise the diagrams are not drawn accurately.

1 Calculate the size of the angles marked by letters.

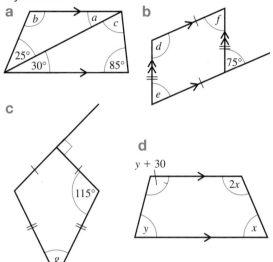

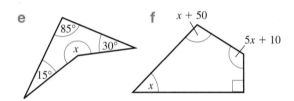

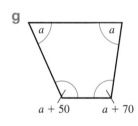

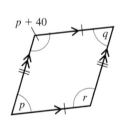

27.3 Exercise A

1 Write down the name of a polygon with
  a five sides
  b six sides
  c eight-sides
  d ten sides

2 A regular heptagon has seven sides. How many lines of symmetry does the heptagon have?

3 A regular dodecagon has 12 sides. Use the circle method to draw a regular dodecagon.

27.3 Exercise B

1 Here are the exterior angles of some polygons.
  Work out the interior angles.
  a 40°   b 100°   c 55°   d 85°

2 Here are the interior angles of some polygons.
  Work out the exterior angles.
  a 130°   b 45°   c 110°   d 15°

3 Here are the interior angles of some regular polygons.
  i Work out the total sum of the interior angles.
  ii Work out the exterior angles.
  a 144° (decagon)
  b 120° (hexagon)
  c 162° (icosagon – 20 sides)

27.4 Exercise A

1 Draw a pentagon. By drawing the diagonals from one vertex, work out the sum of the interior angles of a pentagon.

2 A regular polygon has
  a 6 sides   b 8 sides
  i Calculate the size of the exterior angle.
  ii Calculate the size of the interior angle.

3 Each interior angle of a regular polygon is 144°.
  a Calculate the size of each exterior angle.
  b How many sides does this polygon have?
  c Write down the name of this polygon.

4 Calculate the value of the missing exterior angle of this hexagon.

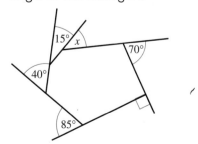

27.4 Exercise B

1 Work out the size of the angle marked with a letter in each of these polygons.

a

b

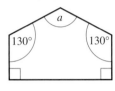

2 The sum of the interior angles of a polygon is 1080°.
How many sides does the polygon have?

3 Work out the size of the angles marked with a letter in each of these polygons.

a   **b**

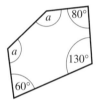 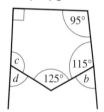

4 A square and an equilateral triangle are joined together as shown.
Calculate the size of angle x.

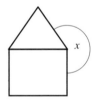

5 Two regular hexagons are joined together as shown.
Calculate the size of angle y.

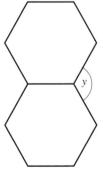

27.5 Exercise A

1 Find the length of the hypotenuse of these triangles.

a   **b**

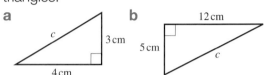

2 Find the length of the hypotenuse of these triangles. Leave each answer as a square root.

a   **b**

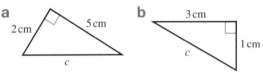

3 Calculate the length of the missing side, marked x, in each of these triangles.

a   **b**

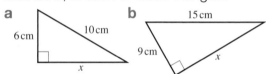

4 Calculate the length of the missing side, marked x, in each of these triangles.
Leave each answer as a square root.

a   **b**

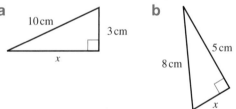

5 Calculate the length of the missing side, marked x, in each of these diagrams. Give each answer to one decimal place.

a   **b**

c   **d**

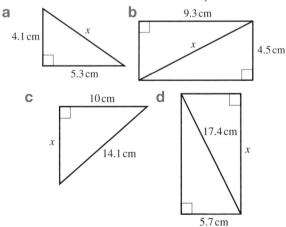

27.5 Exercise B

1 Calculate the vertical height, h, of this isosceles triangle.

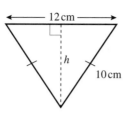

2 A light aircraft is landing. The diagram shows the flight path.
Calculate the value of the distance to touch down, x.

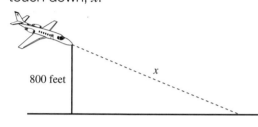

3 Check whether this triangle is right-angled. Show your working.

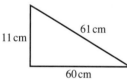

4 Calculate the lengths of x and y in these diagrams.

a

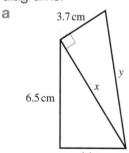

b

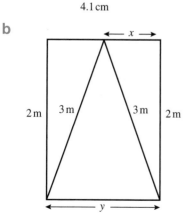

Chapter 28

28.1 Exercise A

1 Write each ratio in its simplest form.
  a $7:14$ b $35:5$ c $20:60$
  d $24:36$ e $18:45$ f $0.3:2.1$
  g $1.5:6$ h $2.7:5.4$ i $1.8:0.9$
  j $3.6:6.6$ k $\frac{1}{2}:6$ l $7:3\frac{1}{2}$
  m $2\frac{1}{4}:4\frac{1}{2}$ n $1:\frac{2}{5}$ o $2\frac{1}{3}:3\frac{2}{3}$

2 In a recipe, flour and butter are mixed in the ratio $3:2$.
The recipe uses 600 g of flour.
How many grams of butter does it use?

3 Which of these ratios are equivalent to $2:5$?

4 Write each ratio in its simplest form.
  a $30:15:60$ b $12:24:36$
  c $9:63:99$ d $13:39:52$
  e $50:500:5000$ f $84:35:14$
  g $4:48:96$ h $6:18:27$

5 The ratio of blue beads to red beads in a bag is $3:7$
There are 56 red beads in the bag.
How many blue beads are in the bag?

28.1 Exercise B

1 **a** Divide £36 in the ratio $5:1$
  b Divide 120 g in the ratio $7:5$
  c Divide 65 litres in the ratio $2:4:7$
  d Divide $150 in the ratio $3:5:7$

2 In each part find the smaller share when
  a $80 is divided in the ratio $1:3$
  b 64 cm is divided in the ratio $7:9$
  c £320 is divided in the ratio $5:3$
  d 81 kg is divided in the ratio $4:5$

3 Ann and Bob share 24 sweets in the ratio 3 : 5
How many more sweets does Bob have than Ann?

4 Green paint is made by mixing blue paint and yellow paint in the ratio 3 : 5
  a If 160 litres of green paint is mixed, how much yellow paint is required?
  b Pete says that to mix 104 litres of green paint he needs 65 litres of blue paint.
  Is he correct? Explain your answer.

5 Linda and Sandra share £315 in the ratio 13 : 8
Sandra says that she received £75 less than Linda.
Is she correct? Show your working.

28.2 Exercise A

1 A fruit bowl contains six apples, three oranges, four pears and one banana.
Write down the proportion of fruit that is
  a oranges   **b** pears
  c **not** apples and **not** bananas

2 Five pencils cost £1.20. Find the cost of
  a one pencil   **b** seven pencils
  c twenty pencils

3 Here is a recipe for a cake for eight people.

| 150 g flour |
| 120 g butter |
| 100 g sugar |
| 3 eggs |

  a How many grams of butter are needed for a recipe for four people?
  b How many grams of sugar are needed for a recipe for six people?
  c How many grams of flour are needed for a recipe for 16 people?

4 Mica receives £76 for her birthday. She saves one quarter and spends the rest.
  a What proportion does she spend?
  b How much does she spend?

5 There are three red marbles out of every seven marbles in a bag.
Altogether there are 35 marbles in the bag.
  a What proportion are red marbles?
  b What proportion are **not** red marbles?
  c How many marbles are **not** red?

28.2 Exercise B

1 Four cans of soft drink cost £1.40
Twelve cans cost £3.99
Which is better value?
Explain your answer.

2 Show that both packets are the same value.

3 Which is the better value?
Show your working.

4 There are 32 565 supporters at a football match one Saturday.
Erin estimates that 1 out of every 15 supporters is a child.
Use Erin's estimate to work out the number of children at the football match.

Chapter 29

29.1 Exercise A

1 If $p = 3$ and $q = 5$, work out
  a $4pq$ **b** $3p + 2q$
  c $p(q - 1)$ **d** $\dfrac{9}{p} + q$

2 If $a = 4$, $b = 5$ and $c = 1$, work out

  a abc **b** $\dfrac{ab}{c}$

  c $\dfrac{a + b}{a - c}$ **d** $(a + b)(b - c)$

3 $A = \dfrac{4x^3}{5}$, $B = 2x(x^2 - 1)$, $C = 2x^2(x + 2)$

Find the values of A, B, and C when $x = 5$

4 If $r = 0.3$, $s = 1.5$ and $t = \frac{1}{2}$ work out

  a rst **b** $\dfrac{1}{r} + \dfrac{1}{s} + \dfrac{1}{t}$

  c $\dfrac{1}{r + s + t}$ **d** $\dfrac{1}{rst}$

29.1 Exercise B

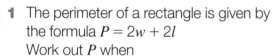

1 The perimeter of a rectangle is given by the formula $P = 2w + 2l$

Work out P when

  a $w = 7$ and $l = 8$
  b $w = 1.5$ and $l = 3.5$
  c $w = 6.7$ and $l = 9.1$
  d $w = 0.52$ and $l = 3.28$

2 The formula $s = \dfrac{(u + v)t}{2}$ is used in the study of motion

  a Work out s when
    i $u = 5$, $v = 7$ and $t = 10$
    ii $u = 10$, $v = 0$ and $t = 5$
  b Work out t when
    i $u = 3$, $v = 8$ and $s = 22$
    ii $u = 5$, $v = 9$ and $s = 7$
  c Work out u when
    i $s = 80$, $v = 5$ and $t = 10$
    ii $s = 6$, $v = 2$ and $t = 3$

3 T is given by the formula $T = \dfrac{ab}{ac + bc}$

Work out T when

  a $a = 4$, $b = 5$ and $c = 8$
  b $a = 3.4$, $b = 5.2$ and $c = 2.8$

4 S is given by the formula $S = \dfrac{x^2 + y^2}{x - y}$

Work out S when

  a $x = 8.5$ and $y = 3.7$
  b $x = 0.42$ and $y = 0.26$

29.2 Exercise A

1 Bags of counters each contain c counters.
  a Write an expression for the number of counters in two bags.
  b Write an expression for the number of counters in two bags when five counters have been removed.
  c Jack bought five bags of counters but lost four counters. Write a formula A for the amount of counters that he has left.

2 Weekly bus tickets cost £14. Monthly bus tickets cost £48
  a Write an expression for the cost of x weekly tickets.
  b Write an expression for the cost of y monthly tickets.
  c Write down a formula for £T, the total cost of x weekly tickets and y monthly tickets.

3 Martine buys four "Healthy snacks" costing h pence each.
She pays with a £10 note and gets £7 change.
Use this information to write an equation in terms of h.

4 Greg is x years old. Luke is y years old.
  a Daniel is three years older than Greg. Write an expression for Daniel's age.
  b Chris is two years younger than Luke. Write an expression for Chris's age.
  c Lynne's age, L, is the sum of Daniel's age and Chris's age. Write a formula giving L in terms of x and y.

5 A company charges £3 for delivering small parcels and £5 for large parcels.
Write a formula for £T, the total amount for delivering s small parcels and l large parcels.

29.2 Exercise B

1 A list of consecutive odd numbers starts
$x, x + 2, x + 4$

  a **i** Copy the list and continue it up to five consecutive odd numbers.

    ii Write down the list when
$x = 13$

  b The sum of three consecutive odd numbers starting with x is 27

    i Use this information to write down an equation in terms of x.

    ii Solve the equation to find the three odd numbers.

2 The diagram shows a shape made up of two rectangles.

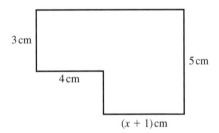

  a Show that the area of this shape, A cm^2, is given by the formula
$A = 5x + 17$

  b Write an equation to find x when
$A = 37$

  c Solve the equation to find x.

3 The table shows the numbers of marbles in six bags labelled A, B, C, D, E and F.
Show that the total number of marbles, T, in all of bags A to F, is $5a + 7b - 7$.

Bag	Number of marbles
A	a
B	b
C	Two more than in bag A
D	Five fewer than in bag B
E	Three times as many as bag C
F	Twice as many as bag D

4 Look at the number machines A and B below.

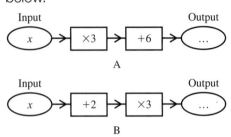

  a Write an expression in terms of x for the output of each machine.

  b Show that the output for machine A equals the output of machine B when the input value, x, is:

    i 5   **ii** 0   **iii** -5

  c Explain your answers to part **b**.

29.3 Exercise A

1 Make x the subject of

  a $y = x + 6$ **b** $w = x - 5$

  c $f = x - g$ **d** $a = b - x$

2 Make x the subject of

  a $c = 4x$ **b** $d = ex$

  c $p = \dfrac{x}{3}$ **d** $q = -\dfrac{x}{r}$

3 Make t the subject of

  a $s = 2t + 7$ **b** $v = 6t - 2$

  c $h = \dfrac{t}{5} + 1$ **d** $j = \dfrac{t}{k} - m$

4 Make n the subject of

  a $a = 8(n + 1)$ **b** $b = n(c - 4)$

  c $d = \dfrac{n + 5}{3}$ **d** $e = \dfrac{n - 6}{f}$

29.3 Exercise B

1 Use the balance method to rearrange each formula in Exercise A.
You **must** show your working.

2 Rearrange the formula $E = mc^2$ to make m the subject.

3 The area of a triangle is given by the formula $A = \frac{1}{2}bh$

   a Calculate A when $b = 12$ cm and $h = 7$ cm.

   b Rearrange the formula to make b the subject.

   c Calculate b when $A = 240$ cm² and $h = 36$ cm.

4 The curved surface area of a cylinder is given by the formula $A = 2\pi rh$.

   a Calculate A when $\pi = 3.14$, $r = 9$ cm and $h = 10$ cm.

   b Rearrange the formula to make h the subject.

   c Calculate h when $A = 100$ cm² and $r = 8.2$ cm. Give your answer to one decimal place.

Chapter 30

30.1 Exercise A

1 1000 cars were observed passing the school gates.
180 of the cars were red.
What is the relative frequency of a red car passing the school gates?
Give your answer as a decimal.

2 The table shows the favourite colours of 50 students.

Colour	Frequency	Relative frequency
Red	14	
White	4	
Blue	18	
Green	8	
Other		

Copy and complete the table.

3 David looks at the first 100 words on the first page of a book.
He counts 34 words that start with a vowel, 29 words that end with a vowel and 13 words that start and end with a vowel.

   a Write down the relative frequency of one of the words

     i starting with a vowel

     ii ending with a vowel

     iii starting and ending with a vowel.

   b Choose a book of your own and repeat David's experiment.
(The word "a" starts, ends and starts and ends with a vowel).

4 In an experiment this trial is repeated 30 times.

● Pick a counter from a bag at random
● Record the number written on the counter.
● Put the counter back in the bag.

The results of the experiment are

```
1  1  4  2  3  1  3  2  5  1
3  4  5  1  3  2  1  4  3  5
4  2  1  3  4  2  4  1  1  2
```

   a Work out the relative frequency of taking a counter from the bag

     i with the number 1 written on it

     ii with a number greater than 3 written on it

     iii with an odd number written on it.

   b Estimate the probability that a counter picked at random from the bag has an even number on it.

30.1 Exercise B

1 The table shows the results when a coin is thrown 50 times.

Number of trials	10	20	30	40	50
Number of heads	4	7	12	18	24
Relative frequency of a head	0.4				

   a Copy and complete the table.

   b Copy and complete the following graph to show how the relative frequency changes as the number of trials increases.

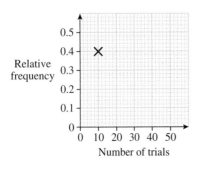

c   Describe the pattern shown in the graph.

2   In an experiment, a bead is taken from a bag at random and its colour is recorded.
The bead is then put back in the bag.
This trial is repeated 500 times.
The table shows the results.

Number of trials	100	200	300	400	500
Number of red beads	42	108	138	176	230

a   Copy and complete this graph to show how the relative frequency of a red bead changes as the number of trials increases.

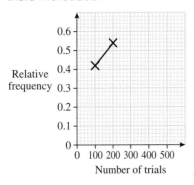

b   Describe the pattern shown in the graph.

3   In an experiment, one of these cards is picked at random and the number recorded.

This trial is repeated 50 times.
The relative frequency of picking 2 is shown in the graph.

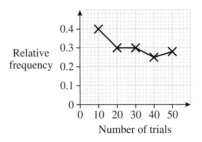

a   Copy and complete the table.

Number of trials	10	20	30	40	50
Relative frequency of 2					

b   Write down the best estimate of the experimental probability of picking a '2'.

c   Compare this with the theoretical probability of picking a '2'.

4   The arrow on a coloured spinner is spun 100 times.
The graph shows the relative frequency of a spinner landing on the colour green at intervals of 10 spins.

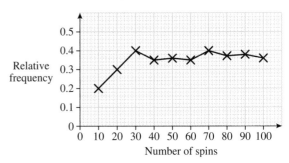

a   Use the graph to calculate the number of times that the arrow lands on green
   i after the first 10 spins
   ii after 100 spins.

b   What is the best estimate of the probability that the spinner lands on green?

30.2 Exercise A

1 Dave rolls an ordinary fair dice 300 times.
Estimate the number of times that Dave is likely to roll a 2

2 Terri spins a coin 10 times and gets 2 heads.
She says the coin is biased.
Sam spins the same coin 200 times and gets 97 heads.
He says the coin is fair.
Who is more likely to be correct?
Explain your answer.

3 The probability of winning a game is 0.2
Tim plays the game 20 times.
Adil plays the game 200 times.
a Estimate the number of times that Tim is likely to win.
b Estimate the number of times that Adil is likely to win.
c Which estimate is more reliable? Explain your answer.

4 A dice was rolled 1500 times.
The results are shown in this table.

Score	1	2	3	4	5	6
Frequency	239	252	256	241	255	257
Relative frequency	0.159					

a Complete the table.
b Is there any evidence to suggest that the dice is biased?
Explain your answer.

5 The arrow on a spinner can land on a red, white or blue sector.
The probability of the spinner landing on each colour is shown in the table.

Colour	Red	White	Blue
Probability	0.4	0.1	0.5

The spinner is spun 150 times.
Estimate the number of times that the spinner lands on each colour.

30.2 Exercise B

1 a A fair coin is thrown thousands of times.
Estimate the relative frequency of throwing a head.
Explain your answer.
b Two fair coins are thrown thousands of times.
Estimate the relative frequency of throwing two heads.
Explain your answer.

2 Mary has a dice with one blue face and five red faces.
She rolls the dice five times and gets three blue faces.
Mary says the dice is biased.
Explain why Mary could be wrong.

3 a James passes a set of traffic lights on his journey to work.
The probability that the lights are at red is 0.4
Estimate the number of times that James does **not** have to stop at the traffic lights in 200 journeys to work.
b In a town, the probability that it will rain on a day in June is 0.1
How many completely dry days are there likely to be in the town during June?

4 A bag contains some red and blue discs.
A disc is taken from the bag at random and its colour is recorded.
The disc is then replaced.
This trial is repeated 500 times.
The table shows the results.

Number of trials	100	200	300	400	500
Number of red discs	42	76	108	138	175

a On a copy of the following grid draw a graph to show how the relative frequency of taking a red disc from the bag changes as the number of trials increases.

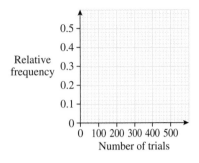

b Estimate the probability of taking a red disc from the bag.

c The bag contains 20 discs. Estimate the number of red discs in the bag.

5 A fair dice has different coloured faces. Yossi, Dovid and Avi each roll the dice for a different number of times and record the colour that the dice lands on.
Their results are shown in the table.

Name	Number of rolls	Colour		
		Red	Blue	Green
Yossi	30	14	12	4
Dovid	120	66	38	16
Avi	300	147	97	56

a What is the relative frequency of rolling a red using the results of
   i Yossi's experiment?
   ii Dovid's experiment?
   iii Avi's experiment?
   iv All three experiments combined?
   In each case, give your answer as a decimal.

b Which of the relative frequencies calculated in part a gives the most reliable estimate of rolling a red? Explain your answer.

c i What is the most likely number of red faces on the dice?
   ii What is the most likely number of blue faces on the dice?
   iii What is the most likely number of green faces on the dice?

Chapter 31

31.1 Exercise A

 1 Work out the area of each of these parallelograms.

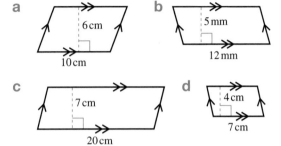

2 Find the area of each of these triangles.

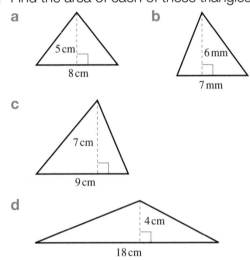

3 Find the area of each of these shapes

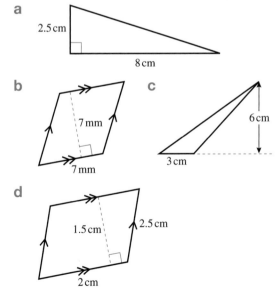

4 Find the area of each of these shapes.

a

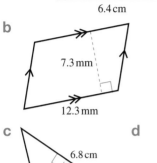

3.1 cm

6.4 cm

b

7.3 mm

12.3 mm

c   **d**

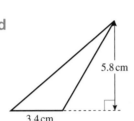

6.8 cm

2.6 cm

5.8 cm

3.4 cm

31.1 Exercise B

 **1** Find the area of each of these shapes.

a   **b**

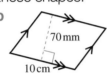

25 mm

10 cm

70 mm

10 cm

c   **d**

6 cm

50 mm

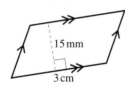

15 mm

3 cm

2 Which of these shapes has the largest area?
Show your working.

a

5 cm

8 cm

b

6 mm

7 mm

c

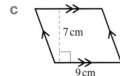

7 cm

9 cm

 3 A triangle has an area of 10 cm² and a perpendicular height of 4 cm.
A parallelogram has an area of 10 cm² and a perpendicular height of 4 cm.
Which of the shapes has the longest base? Show your working.

4 Which of these shapes is the odd one out?
Show your working.

a

2.5 cm

60 mm

b

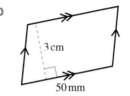

3 cm

50 mm

c

25 mm

12 cm

d

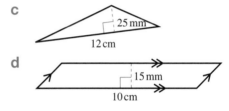

15 mm

10 cm

31.2 Exercise A

 1 Draw and label a circle to show

a	the circumference	**b**	a radius
c	a diameter	**d**	a chord
e	a tangent	**f**	an arc
g	a segment	**h**	a sector.

2 a What is the special name for the perimeter of a circle?

b Which part of a circle is described by each of the following statements?

i A straight line from the centre of a circle to a point on its edge.

ii A straight line joining different points on the edge of a circle that passes through the centre.

iii A straight line joining different points on the edge of a circle that does **not** pass through the centre.

iv A straight line that touches the edge of a circle.

3 Estimate the circumferences of these circles. Take π to be 3

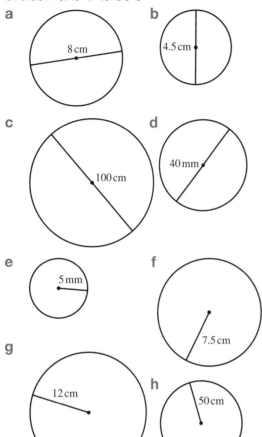

a 8 cm

b 4.5 cm

c 100 cm

d 40 mm

e 5 mm

f 7.5 cm

g 12 cm

h 50 cm

4 Calculate the circumference of each of the circles in question **3**
Leave your answer in terms of π

5 a Write down the value of π to two decimal places.
   b Measure the diameter of a 2 pence coin to the nearest millimetre.
   Use your value of π from part **a** to work out the circumference of the 2 pence coin.
   Give your answer to one decimal place.

31.2 Exercise B

1 In this question take π to be 3
   a Estimate the diameter of a circle of circumference 36 cm.
   b Estimate the radius of a circle of circumference 27 mm.

2 In his garden, Mr Jones has a circular fish pond.
The diameter of the pond is 3.5 m.
Mr Jones wants to put a fence around the edge of the pond.
Calculate the length of fencing that he needs to do this.
Give your answer in terms of π.

 In questions **3** to **5**, use $\pi = 3.14$ or the π button on your calculator.

3 Find the perimeter of this shape.

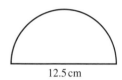

12.5 cm

4 a A circle has circumference 23.1 cm. Calculate its diameter to one decimal place.
   b A circle has circumference 17.6 mm. Calculate its radius to two decimal places.

5 The wheel of a car has a diameter of 62 cm.
Calculate the number of complete revolutions made by the wheel when the car travels 1 kilometre.
(1 km = 100 000 cm)

31.3 Exercise A

1 Estimate the area of the following circles. Take π to be 3

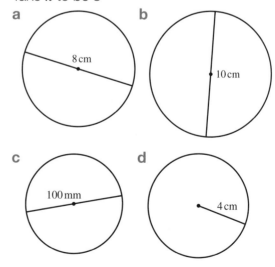

a 8 cm

b 10 cm

c 100 mm

d 4 cm

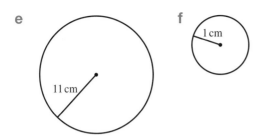

e 11 cm

f 1 cm

2 Calculate the area of each of the circles in question **1**
Leave your answer in terms of π

In questions **3** and **4**, use $\pi = 3.14$ or the π button on your calculator.

3 Calculate the area of the following circles. Give your answer to two decimal places.

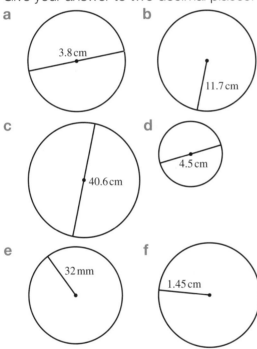

a 3.8 cm

b 11.7 cm

c 40.6 cm

d 4.5 cm

e 32 mm

f 1.45 cm

4 A £1 coin has a diameter of 13 mm.
Calculate the total area of both faces of the coin.
Give your answer to one decimal place.

31.3 Exercise B

1 Calculate the area of each of the following shapes. Leave your answer in terms of π.

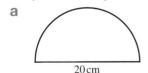

a 20 cm

b 8 cm

2 The diagram shows a circular pond of diameter 4 metres.
It is surrounded by a path of width 1 metre.

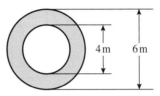

4 m   6 m

Estimate the area of the path (shown shaded in the diagram).
Take π to be 3

In questions **3** and **4**, use $\pi = 3.14$ or the π button on your calculator.

3 A shape is made by cutting out a quarter of a circle from each corner of a rectangle.
The rectangle is 4 cm long and 3 cm wide.
The radius of the quarter circle is 1 cm.

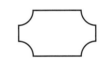

a Calculate the area of the shape.

b This pattern is made from six of the shapes.

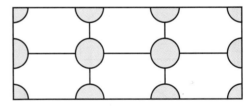

Calculate the shaded area.

4 A table top is made from four semi circles fixed to the sides of a square.

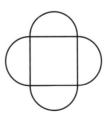

The square has sides of length 1.2 metres.
Find the area of the table top.

31.4 Exercise A

1 Work out the perimeter of each of these shapes.

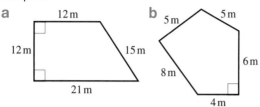

a

b

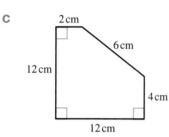

c

2 Work out the area of each of these shapes.

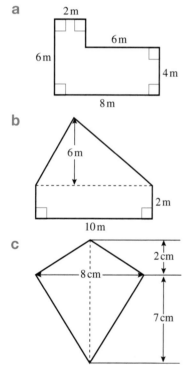

a

b

c

3 Calculate the area of each trapezium.

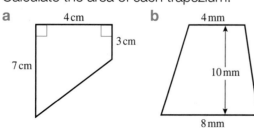

a

b

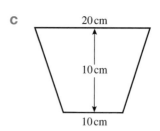

c

4 Calculate the area of each of these shapes.

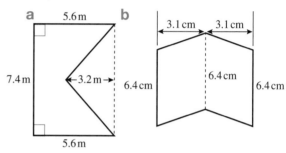

a

b

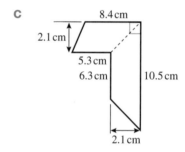

c

31.4 Exercise B

1 Calculate the area of each of these shapes.

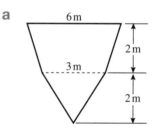

a

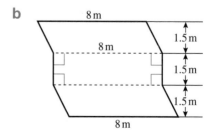

b

2 Calculate the shaded area.

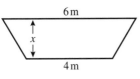

3 a The area of this trapezium is 10 cm². Calculate, x, the perpendicular height of the trapezium.

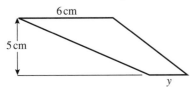

b The area of this trapezium is 20 cm².

Calculate the length if the base of the trapezium (marked y on the diagram).

4 Calculate the shaded area in each of these shapes.

a

b

5 The diagram shows the floor of an L-shaped room.

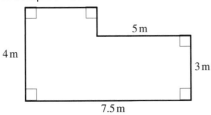

David is planning to buy carpet tiles for the floor.
The carpet tiles cost £9.60 per square metre.
Work out the cost of tiling the floor.

Chapter 32

32.1 Exercise A

Solve the following equations.

1 a $2a + 8 = 0$ **b** $3b - 16 = -7$

   c $5c - 3 = -8$ **d** $\dfrac{d}{4} + 4 = 2$

   e $\dfrac{e}{5} - 3 = -2$ **f** $\dfrac{f}{2} + 7 = 1$

2 a $3a + 9 = 2a + 1$
   b $7b - 1 = 5b + 7$
   c $8c - 1 = 3c + 9$
   d $6d + 12 = 4d - 3$
   e $8e - 8 = 3e - 2$
   f $7f + 2 = 3f + 8$

3 a $5(a + 1) = 4a - 6$
   b $3(2b - 5) = 4b - 7$
   c $3(5c + 3) = 5c + 3$
   d $3(2d - 6) = 2 - 4d$
   e $5(2e - 2) = 2e - 2$
   f $4(3f - 2) = 8f + 6$

4 a $4(a - 3) + 3 = 3a + 6$
   b $3(4b - 1) - 3 = 2b - 13$
   c $2(5c - 3) = 5(c + 1) + 4$
   d $6(2d - 1) - 8d = 3(d + 1)$
   e $5(2e - 3) + 4(e - 2) = 4(3e - 1)$
   f $3(7f - 3) - 2 - 2f = 4f + 19$

32.1 Exercise B

1 Form and solve an equation to find x in each of the following triangles.

a

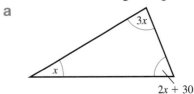

b

3x + 23

x   37°

c   3x − 7

2x − 4

x − 1

2 Form and solve an equation to find y in each of the following diagrams.

a

2y + 30

2y

y

b   2y + 12

3(y + 5)

95°

y − 17

3 Tom and Sally are investigating the numbers they can make using these rules.

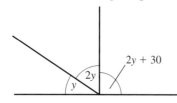

I think of a number. I multiply it by 4 and subtract 3. My answer is.......

I think of a number. I multiply it by 2 and then add 5. My answer is.......

Using x to represent the numbers that Tom and Sally think of, write down an equation in x and then solve it to find

a   the number Tom thinks of when his answer is 13

b   the number Sally thinks of when her answer is 27

c   the number that Tom and Sally think of when they both think of the same number and get the same answer.

4 In bag A there are x counters.
In bag B there are two more counters than in bag A.
In bag C there are three times as many counters as there are in bag B.
In bag D there are four times as many counters as there are in bag A.
The number of counters in bag D equals the number of counters in bag C.
Calculate the value of x.

5 Rectangle A has sides with dimensions 5 cm and $(2x − 1)$ cm.
Rectangle B has sides with dimensions 3 cm and $(2x + 1)$ cm.

a   Work out x if the perimeter of rectangle A is 16 cm.

b   Work out x if the area of rectangle B is 18 cm².

c   Work out x if the area of rectangle B equals the area of rectangle A.

32.2 Exercise A

1 Rewrite each of the following statements using inequality symbols.

a a is greater than 5

b b is less than or equal to 1

c c is greater than or equal to −3

d d is less than 4

2 Show the following inequalities on a copy of this number line.
Use a different number line for each inequality.

```
├──┼──┼──┼──┼──┼──┼──┼──┼──┼──┼──┼──┤
-6 -5 -4 -3 -2 -1  0  1  2  3  4  5  6
```

a $x < 2$ **b** $x \geqslant 2$ **c** $x > -1$

d $x \leqslant -3$ **e** $-2 > x$ **f** $-4 \leqslant x$

g $2 \geqslant x$ **h** $2 < x$

3 The number lines show values of x.
Write down each of the inequalities.

a

b

c

-6 -5 -4 -3 -2 -1 0 1 2 3 4 5 6

d

-6 -5 -4 -3 -2 -1 0 1 2 3 4 5 6

4 Solve each of the following inequalities.
a	$a + 2 \leqslant 1$	**b**	$b - 5 > -1$
c	$4c \geqslant 12$	**d**	$\frac{1}{4}d < -3$
e	$2e + 3 \leqslant -1$	**f**	$4f < 2f + 12$

5
a	$a - 3 > -7$	**b**	$b - 5 \leqslant -2$
c	$3c < -12$	**d**	$\frac{1}{3}d \geqslant -1$
e	$3e - 2 \leqslant -5$	**f**	$6f > 2f - 8$
g	$\frac{1}{5}g - 3 \geqslant -2$		

32.2 Exercise B

1 a Ken says that the integers -1, 0, 1 fit the double inequality $-2 \leqslant x < 1$
Explain why Ken is wrong.
b Kay says that the integers -2, 0, 1 and 2 fit the inequalities $-2 \geqslant x$ and $x \geqslant 2$
Explain why Kay is wrong.

2 You are given the following inequalities

$$W \quad -3 \leqslant x < 2$$
$$X \quad -2 < x \leqslant 4$$
$$Y \quad x < 1 \text{ or } x \geqslant 5$$
$$Z \quad x < 0 \text{ or } x > 4$$

a Show each of inequalities W, X, Y and Z on a number line.
b Write down the integers that fit both inequality W and inequality X.
c Write down the integers that fit both inequality W and inequality Y.

d Write down the integers that fit all of the inequalities W, X, Y and Z.

3 Write down the inequalities shown on each of these number lines.

a
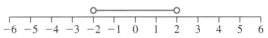

b

-6 -5 -4 -3 -2 -1 0 1 2 3 4 5 6

c

-6 -5 -4 -3 -2 -1 0 1 2 3 4 5 6

4 a Write the following pairs of inequalities as a single inequality.
i $-3 < x$ and $x \leqslant 2$
ii $-4 \leqslant x$ and $x < 3$
iii $0 \leqslant x$ and $x \leqslant 4$
iv $-3 < x$ and $x < 3$
b Write down two separate inequalities that are equivalent to these double inequalities.
i	$-2 \leqslant x \leqslant 4$	**ii**	$-4 \leqslant x < 1$
iii	$-2 < x \leqslant 3$	**iv**	$-5 < x < 2$

c List the integers contained in each of the inequalities in **a** and **b**.

5 Solve each of the following inequalities.
a $-2 \leqslant x + 2 < 3$
b $-3 \leqslant x - 5 \leqslant -1$
c $-6 < 2x < 8$
d $-15 \leqslant 5x < 5$
e $-1 \leqslant \frac{1}{2}x \leqslant 2$
f $-3 < \frac{1}{4}x \leqslant 1$

32.3 Exercise A

1 Each of the following equations has a solution that is a whole number.
Use the method of trial and improvement to find each solution.
You **must** show your trials.
a $a^2 + a = 30$
b $b^3 - 2b^2 = 75$
c $c^3 + 5c = 84$

2 Tom, Matthew and Emmie are solving an equation using trial and improvement.

  a Tom finds that the solution lies between $x = 4.5$ and $x = 5$

    What is the solution to the nearest whole number?

  b Matthew finds that the solution lies between $x = 4.7$ and $x = 4.75$

    What is the solution to one decimal place?

  c Emmie finds that the solution lies between $x = 4.72$ and $x = 4.73$

    i Write this information as an inequality.

    ii What value of x should Emmie try so that she can give the solution to two decimal places?

3 **a** The solution of the equation $x^3 - x = 80$ lies between $x = p$ and $x = q$ where p and q are consecutive whole numbers.

    i Find the values of p and q.

    ii Write this information as an inequality.

  b Repeat part **a** for

    i $x^3 - x^2 = 30$ **ii** $x^3 + 2x^2 = 120$

 4 Copy and complete the following to solve the equation $x^3 + x = 50$ using the method of trial and improvement.

Give your answer to an accuracy of one decimal place.

Trial value of x	$x^3 + x = ...$	Comment	Conclusion
3	$3^3 + 3 = ...$	Too ...	$x > 3$
4	...	...	$... < x < ...$

The solution lies between $x = ...$ and $x = ...$

Trial value of x	$x^3 + x = ...$	Comment	Conclusion
3.5	$3.5^3 + 3.5 = ...$	...	$... < x < ...$
...	...	...	$... < x < ...$

The solution lies between $x = ...$ and $x = ...$

Trial value of x	$x^3 + x = ...$	Comment	Conclusion
...	...	...	$... < x < ...$

So to one decimal place the solution of $x^3 + x = 20$ is $x = ...$

5 Use trial and improvement to solve the following equations.

Use the starting values given.

Give each of your answers to one decimal place.

You **must** show your trials.

  a $a^2 + a = 80$ (start with $a = 8$)

  b $b^3 - 2b = 35$ (start with $a = 3$)

32.3 Exercise B

 1 Use trial and improvement to solve the following equations.

Use the starting values given.

Give each of your answers to one decimal place.

You **must** show your trials.

  a $a^2 - \sqrt{a} = 95$ (start with $a = 9$)

  b $b^3 - b^2 = 55$ (start with $b = 3$)

  c $c^3 + c^2 - c = 5$ (start with $c = 1$)

  d $d^3 - d^2 - \dfrac{1}{d} = 145$ (start with $d = 5$)

2 Use trial and improvement to solve the following equations.

Give each of your answers to one decimal place.

You **must** show your trials.

  a $a^3 - 5a = 200$ **b** $b^3 - 3b^2 = 6$

  c $c^3 + 4c = 120$

  d $d^3 - 2d^2 + 5d = 42$

Chapter 33

33.1 Exercise A

 1 Each of the following values is given to the nearest whole number.

Write down the largest and smallest possible values.

  a £8   **b** £15   **c** £200

  d 40 kg   **e** 32 m   **f** 2 minutes

2 Write down the minimum and maximum values of each of the following.
  a £20 to the nearest pound
  b 80 pence to the nearest 10p
  c £200 to the nearest £10
  d 55 pence to the nearest 5p

3 a Write down the minimum and maximum values of each of the following.
    i 100 miles to the nearest mile
    ii 100 miles to the nearest 5 miles
    iii 100 miles to the nearest 10 miles
  b Write down the minimum and maximum values of each of the following.
    i 60 metres to the nearest metre
    ii 60 metres to the nearest 5 metres
    iii 60 metres to the nearest 10 metres

4 The attendance at a Premier league football match was 52 000 to the nearest 1 000
What was the smallest possible attendance?

5 The attendance at a basketball match was 3 450 to the nearest 50
What was the smallest possible attendance?

33.1 Exercise B

1 Write each of the following values to a suitable degree of accuracy, giving a reason for your answer.
  a The average height of the boys in a class is 153.2 cm.
  b The distance between Newcastle and London is 465.7 km.
  c The average shoe size of the girls in a class is 4.2

2 Write each of these measures to an appropriate degree of accuracy.
  a The length of the River Nile is 4184 miles.
  b The diameter of the Earth is 7926.2 miles.

c The estimated population of the USA on 11th of October, 2006 was 299 954 638

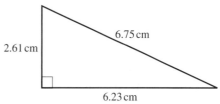

3 Each length on this triangle is approximate.

  a Work out the perimeter of the triangle. Give your answer to a suitable degree of accuracy.
  b Work out the area of the triangle. Give your answer to a suitable degree of accuracy.

4 a This formula converts temperature in degrees Fahrenheit (°F) to degrees Celsius (°C).

$$C = \frac{F - 32}{1.8}$$

Convert 61° F to degrees Celsius. Give your answer to a suitable degree of accuracy.

  b This formula converts temperature in degrees Celsius (°C) to degrees Fahrenheit (°F).

$F = 1.8C + 32$

Convert −4°C to degrees Fahrenheit. Give your answer to a suitable degree of accuracy.

33.2 Exercise A

1 Write the following times as fractions of an hour.
  a 6 minutes   **b** 18 minutes
  c 9 minutes   **d** 3 hours 45 minutes

2 a Work out the average speed for these journeys in kilometres per hour.
    i 90 kilometres in 3 hours
    ii 50 kilometres in 2 hours
    iii 100 kilometres in 5 hours

b Work out the average speed for these journeys in metres per second.

    i 50 metres in 10 seconds

    ii 600 metres in 20 seconds

    iii 1 kilometre in 100 seconds

3 Work out the average speed for these journeys.

Give your answer in miles per hour.

a 25 miles in $\frac{1}{2}$ hour

b 10 miles in 10 minutes

c 15 miles in 20 minutes

d 30 miles in 45 minutes

4 The fastest species of fish is the Indo-Pacific Sailfish.

At its fastest it can swim 60 metres in 5 seconds.

What is this speed in metres per second?

 5 Work out the average speed for these journeys.

Give your answer in kilometres per hour.

a 60 kilometres in $1\frac{1}{2}$ hours

b 80 kilometres in 1 hour 20 minutes

c 4.6 kilometres in 3 minutes

d 48 kilometres in 45 minutes

33.2 Exercise B

 1 Work out the distance travelled at an average speed of

a 60 mph for 3 hours

b 80 km/h for 5 hours

c 24 m/s for 10 seconds

d 70 mph for 30 minutes

e 40 km/h for 6 minutes

f 60 mph for 1 minute

2 Work out the time taken, in minutes, to travel

a 10 miles at 20 mph

b 40 miles at 40 mph

c 30 miles at 15 mph

d 20 kilometres at 100 km/h

e 120 kilometres at 50 km/h

f 150 kilometres at 40 km/h

3 The distance between two stations is 15 kilometres.

A train travels between the stations in 10 minutes.

a What is the average speed of the train in kilometres per hour?

b Explain why the top speed of the train is greater than its average speed.

 4 a A person travels 50 miles in 2 hours and then a further 40 miles in 1 hour. Calculate the average speed for the whole journey.

b A person travels 100 miles at an average speed of 40 mph.

    i How long was the journey? Give your answer in hours and minutes.

    ii In the first two hours of the journey the average speed was 35 mph. What was the average speed for the remainder of the journey?

Chapter 34

34.1 Exercise A

 1 The following questions are about revising for exams.

Which of them are

a too open? **b** closed? **c** leading?

Question 1

How much time do you spend revising?

Question 2

How much time did you spend revising last night?

Tick a box for your answer.

Less than 1 hour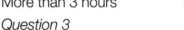

Between 1 and 2 hours

Between 2 and 3 hours

More than 3 hours

Question 3

Revising means you will do better in exams.

What do you think?

2 a Write down **one** thing that is wrong with each of these questions.

    i How much do you spend on DVDs?

    ii Coronation Street is the best TV soap, isn't it?

    iii What sort of TV programmes do you like to watch and why?

    iv What is your bed-time?

b In each case write a better question to find out the same information.

3 Write suitable response sections for each of these questions.

    a What size shoes do you wear?

    b What is your favourite TV reality show?

    c How often do you play football each week?

4 Write a question to find out the following. Give a response section where appropriate.

    a The total number of rooms in different houses.

    b How students travel to school.

    c How often students go to the cinema.

    d What pupils eat for breakfast.

5 a Design a short questionnaire on one of the following topics:

    i Pets

    ii Homework

    iii Exercise

    b Use your questionnaire in a pilot survey of about five people.

    c Use the results of your pilot survey to improve your questionnaire where necessary.

34.1 Exercise B

1 Explain the meaning of these terms.

    a Population   **b** Sample

    c Census

    d Representative sample

2 In a school, year 10 and year 11 are considering whether to have a separate or combined Christmas disco.

In year 10, 10% of the students are asked for their opinion about this.

In year 11, all of the students are asked for their opinion.

    a Which year group is carrying out a census?

    Explain your answer.

    b Give one advantage and one disadvantage of year 10's approach.

    c Give one advantage and one disadvantage of year 11's approach.

3 A school is thinking of changing its school uniform.

They decide to survey the opinion of the pupils in the school.

    a Write down some questions that the school could ask in a questionnaire.

    b Describe how they could choose a sample of pupils to complete the questionnaire.

4 Chandni wants to survey people in her school about their reading habits.

    a Write a questionnaire that would enable Chandni to investigate

        i the sort of things that pupils in her school read for pleasure

        ii how often and for how long they read for pleasure.

    b Chandni considers the following ways of choosing pupils to complete her questionnaire.

    Method 1

    Ask pupils in her maths group.

    Method 2

    Go to the school library at lunch time and ask the first ten people that she meets.

    Method 3

    Ask her family and friends.

    Method 4

    Ask one boy and one girl from every class in the school.

    Comment on each of the methods she is considering.

34.2 Exercise A

1 Terri was investigating favourite breakfast cereals.
She wanted to know if it was different for adults and children.

   a Design an observation sheet to collect this information.

   b Complete the observation sheet for five adults and five children.

2 a Design an observation sheet to collect information about the meals sold to boys and girls in the school canteen.

   b Invent the first 20 entries.

3 Tim is doing a survey on the amount of time students spend doing homework on different days.
He designs this observation sheet.

Time, hours	0–1	1–2	2–3	>3
Monday				
Tuesday				
Wednesday				
Thursday				
Friday				

   a Criticise and improve Tim's observation sheet.

   b What question should Tim ask to help him complete his improved sheet?

4 a Describe how data logging might be used to collect data about the number of people there are in a shop at different times.

   b How might this data be useful to the shop's manager?

34.2 Exercise B

1 Dipak is organising a school trip for his class.
He asks each student in his class to choose if they would like to go to the beach, the zoo or a theme park.
This is how he recorded his results.

Beach	Zoo	Zoo
Theme Park	Zoo	Theme Park
Theme Park	Theme Park	Zoo
Zoo	Zoo	Zoo
Beach	Zoo	Theme Park
Zoo	Zoo	Theme Park
Theme Park	Zoo	Theme Park
Beach	Zoo	Beach
Theme Park	Beach	Zoo
Zoo	Theme Park	

   a Design an observation sheet that would improve Dipak's method of data collection.

   b Use Dipak's data to complete your observation sheet.

   c Where did the students in Dipak's class prefer to go on their trip?

2 Sarah does a survey to try and find out if students who live close to school are more likely to walk to school.
Here is her completed observation sheet.

Distance, km	Up to 1	More than 1 and up to 2	More than 2 and up to 3	More than 3
Walk	IIII III	IIII	III	
Don't walk	III	IIII II	IIII II	III

   a State whether each of these statements about the observation sheet are true or false.
Give a reason each time.

     i Students who live close to school are likely to walk to school.

     ii Most students walk to school.

   b Design an observation sheet to investigate whether boys or girls are more likely to walk to school.

3 The telephone switchboard in a school takes calls between 8 am and 5 pm.
A data logging machine records information about the number of telephone calls to the school on a Monday and a Tuesday.

Time	Number of calls	
	Monday	Tuesday
Before 9 am	12	8
Before 10 am	23	22
Before 11 am	32	29
Before 12 am	46	44
Before 1 pm	62	58
Before 2 pm	68	62
Before 3 pm	74	70
Before 4 pm	86	84
Before 5 pm	93	95

a On which day were there more telephone calls? How many more?

b How many calls were there between 9 am and 10 am on Monday?

c Which day had the most telephone calls in the morning?

d Which day had the least number of telephone calls in the afternoon?

e In which hour was there the greatest number of calls on Monday?

f In which hour was there the least number of calls on Monday and Tuesday?

34.3 Exercise A

1 The percentage increase in the price of food from 1995 to 2000 was 20%. If the index number for food in 1995 is 100, what is the index number for food in 2000?

2 The index number for clothing in 2003 was 110 using 2000 as the base year. Anna spent £500 on clothes in 2000 She buys the same sort of clothes in 2003 How much does she spend in 2003?

3 In 1991 a house in Newcastle was valued at £93 500

In 2006 the same house was valued at £320 000 Find the index number for this house in 2006 using 1991 as the base.

4 In 1901 the population of the United Kingdom was 38 323 000
a The population in 1951 was 50 290 000 Find the index number for 1951 using 1901 as the base year.
b Using 1951 as the base year the index number for 2001 is 117.3 Calculate the population of the United Kingdom in 2001 Give your answer to the nearest 1000

5 The table shows the average price (to the nearest £50) of a house in Britain every 10 years from 1940 to 2000

Year	1940	1950	1960	1970
Price, £	750	2 000	2 800	6 750

Year	1980	1990	2000
Price, £	22 000	55 700	111 050

a Draw a time series graph for the data.
b Describe any patterns in the data.
c In which decade was the least increase in house prices?
d Using 1960 as the base what is the index number in
   i 2000   ii 1940?

34.3 Exercise B

1 Copy and complete the table using 1990 as the base year.

Product	1990		2000	
	Price, p	Index	Price, p	Index
Bread	40	100	60	
Beer	200	100	220	
Toothbrushes	100	100		75
Newspapers	50	100		120

2 This table shows the average wages of workers in the manufacturing industry in 1970 and 1994 together with the average cost of typical purchases.

Year	1970	1994
Average wages, £ per year	345	2 029
Average costs, £ per year	230	1 748

a Using 1970 as the base year work out the index numbers for both average wages and average costs of purchases.

b In which year were workers in the manufacturing industry better off?

3 The table shows index numbers for the average cost of different items in 1995 taking 1993 as the base year.

Goods	Mortgage	Heating and lighting	Clothing	Food	Other items
Index number	110	130	95	115	120

a Which of the items had the smallest percentage change between 1993 and 1995?

b Which of the items decreased in price between 1993 and 1995?

c In 1993, Matthew paid an average of £40 per month for his gas bill. If gas prices moved in line with average prices for heating and lighting, what is Matthew's average monthly gas bill in 1995?

d What would cost more in 1995?
● Food purchases in a supermarket costing £85 in 1993
● Clothing purchases costing £106 in 1993
Assume that each item's price moved according to the index number in the table.

Chapter 35

35.1 Exercise A

1 Draw the plan view of each shape accurately on centimetre squared paper.

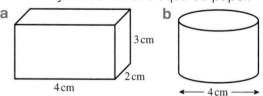

a

b

2 Draw a sketch of
a the plan view of this shape
b its side elevation
c its front elevation.

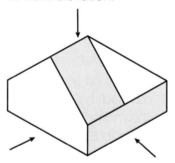

3 Each of these solids is made from centimetre cubes.
For each solid draw on centimetre squared paper
i the plan view
ii the view from A
iii the view from B

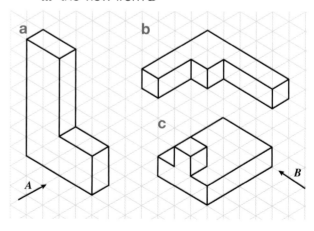

a

b

c

4 The plan view, front elevation and side elevation of a 3-D solid made from cubes are as shown.
Draw the solid on isometric paper.

Plan view	Front elevation	Side elevation
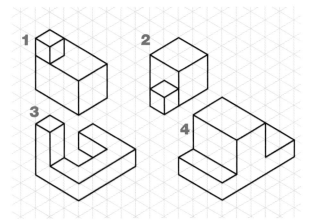		

35.1 Exercise B

Each of the following solids is made from different sized cubes and/or cuboids.
For each solid

a Draw the plan view, front elevation and side elevation on centimetre squared paper.

b Calculate the surface area.

c Calculate the volume.

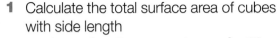

35.2 Exercise A

1 Calculate the total surface area of cubes with side length

   a 1 cm **b** 5 cm **c** 4 cm **d** 20 cm

2 For each of these cuboids sketch the net and then calculate the total surface area.

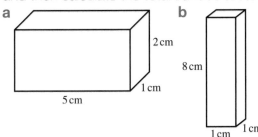

3 The diagram shows a triangular prism.

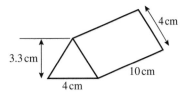

a Sketch a net of the prism.

b Calculate the total surface area of the prism.

4 Calculate the curved surface area of each of these cylinders.
Leave your answer in terms of π.

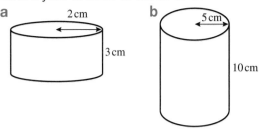

5 a Calculate the total surface area of a cube with side length 3.72 cm.

b A cuboid has length 6.3 cm, width 4.8 cm and height 8.5 cm.
Calculate its total surface area.

c Calculate the total surface area of a cylinder with radius 4.6 cm and height 8.3 cm.

35.2 Exercise B

1 a Convert the following areas to square metres

   i 23 500 cm²   **ii** 4 520 cm²

b Convert the following areas to square centimetres

   i 5 m²   **ii** 0.4 m²

2 A cuboid measures 10 mm by 5 mm by 2 mm.
Calculate the total surface area of the cuboid.

a Give your answer in mm².

b Convert your answer to part **a** into cm².

3 Calculate the surface area of this wedge shape.

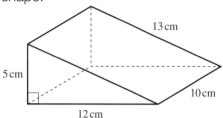

4 a Cylinder *A* has radius 5.6 cm and height 7.2 cm.
Cylinder *B* has diameter 5.6 cm and height 14.4 cm.
Which cylinder has the greatest total surface area?

b Cylinder *C* has diameter 1 cm and height 1 cm.
Show that Cylinder *C* has a smaller total surface area than a cube of side length 1 cm.

35.3 Exercise A

1 The diagram shows a triangular prism.

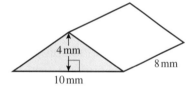

a Sketch the cross-section.
b Work out the area of the cross-section.
c Work out the volume of the prism. State the units of your answer.

2 Calculate an estimate of the volume of a cylinder of radius 10 cm and height 20 cm.
Take the value of π to be 3
State the units of your answer.

3 Work out the volume of each of these prisms.

a

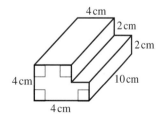

b

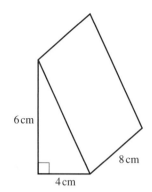

4 Work out the volume of each of these cylinders.

a

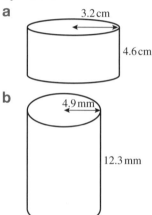

b

35.3 Exercise B

1 a Convert the following volumes to cubic metres (m^3)
    i 1 825 500 cm^3 **ii** 55 000 000 cm^3
b Convert the following volumes to cubic centimetres (cm^3)
    i 6.5 m^3 **ii** 0.2 m^3

2 Does a cuboid with dimensions 15 cm by 10 cm by 8 cm hold more or less than 1 litre?
Give a reason for your answer.

3 The diagram shows a cylinder.
The volume of the cylinder is 500π cm^3.
The radius of the cylinder is 10 cm.
Calculate the height of the cylinder.

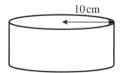

4 A 4 pint container of milk contains 2.727 litres.
The container is used to fill mugs of diameter 7.8 cm to a height of 7.5 cm.

a How many mugs can be filled from one carton of milk?

b How many cartons of milk are required to fill 20 mugs?

Chapter 36

36.1 Exercise A

1 Write down the first five terms of the sequences with the nth terms below. Describe each sequence in words.

a $3n$

b $2n + 7$

c $4n + 1$

d $5n - 1$

2 a A sequence has nth term $3n - 5$. Find the

  i 5th term

  ii 10th term

  iii 20th term.

b Another sequence has nth term $10n - 9$. Find the

  i 100th term

  ii 200th term

  iii 300th term.

3 Look at these nth terms

| $2n + 9$ | $5n + 2$ | $4n - 3$ |

| $7n + 8$ | $n + 16$ |

a Which two sequences have a term equal to 19?

b Which sequence does **not** have a term equal to 17?

c Which two sequences have all odd number terms?

d Which three sequences have the term 22 in common?

e Which sequence has the term to term rule 'add 7'?

4 a **i** Use the number machine to complete the table.

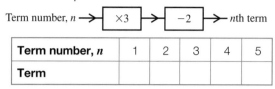

Term number, n → ×3 → −2 → nth term

Term number, n	1	2	3	4	5
Term					

  ii What is the term to term rule for the sequence?

  iii Find the nth term for the sequence. Repeat part **a** for the sequences given by these number machines

b

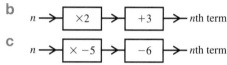

n → ×2 → +3 → nth term

c

n → × −5 → −6 → nth term

36.1 Exercise B

1 A sequence has nth term $3n - 5$
What is the constant difference between consecutive terms of this sequence?

2 A sequence has nth term $3n$.
Which of the following numbers cannot be in the sequence?

9   13   15   18   20   23   24

Explain your answer.

3 a A sequence has nth term $n^2 + 3$

  i Write down the first five terms of the sequence.

  ii Describe the pattern of differences between consecutive terms.

Repeat part **a** for the sequences with nth terms

b $n^2 - 6$ **c** $n(n + 4)$

d $(n - 2)^2$ **e** $2n^2 + 5$

4 Is 50 a term in the sequence with nth term $2n^2$? Explain your answer.

36.2 Exercise A

1 Write down the nth term of each of the following sequences

a 4, 8, 12, 16, 20, …

b 9, 18, 27, 36, 45, …

c $1\frac{1}{2}$, 3, $4\frac{1}{2}$, 6, $7\frac{1}{2}$, …

d −6, −12, −18, −24, −30, …

2 Write down the nth term of each of the following sequences
  a 7, 12, 17, 22, 27, ...
  b −3, 2, 7, 12, 17, ...
  c 9, 11, 13, 15, 17, ...
  d −8, −1, 6, 13, 20, ...
  e 50, 42, 34, 26, 18, ...
  f 21, 17.5, 14, 10.5, 7, ...

3 These patterns are made from dots

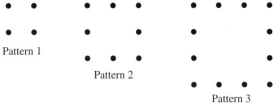

Pattern 1

Pattern 2

Pattern 3

  a Find an expression for the number of dots in Pattern n.
  b How many dots form Pattern 50?
  c Which pattern in the sequence has 628 dots?

4 These rhombus patterns are made from matchsticks.

rhombus   2 rhombuses   3 rhombuses

Copy and complete this table

Number of rhombuses	1	2	3	4	n		86
Number of matchsticks						157	

36.2 Exercise B

1 The sequence 1, 4, 9, 16, 25, ... has nth term n^2.
Use this to write down the nth term of the following sequences
  a 3, 12, 27, 48, 75, ...
  b 2, 5, 10, 17, 26, ...
  c −3, 0, 5, 12, 21, ...
  d 20, 80, 180, 320, 500, ...

2 Write down the nth term of each of the following sequences
  a $2 \times 3, 3 \times 6, 4 \times 9, 5 \times 12, ...$
  b $2 \times 2, 6 \times 4, 10 \times 6, 14 \times 8, ...$

c $\frac{1}{8}, \frac{4}{10}, \frac{9}{12}, \frac{16}{14}, \frac{25}{16}, ...$
d $\frac{10}{20}, \frac{13}{17}, \frac{16}{14}, \frac{19}{11}, \frac{22}{8}, ...$

3 a Two sequences have nth terms $8n - 1$ and $6n + 9$
  i Which term of each sequence makes them equal to each other?
  ii What is the value of this term?
  b Explain why the sequences $3n + 4$ and $5n - 7$ do **not** have a term in common.

4 a Find the nth term of 1, 4, 9, 16, 25, ...
  b Find the nth term of 3, 6, 9, 12, 15, ...
  c Use your answers to **a** and **b** to find the nth terms of
  i 4, 10, 18, 28, 40
  ii −2, −2, 0, 4, 10

Chapter 37

37.1 Exercise A

1 Write down all the prime numbers less than 20

2 Copy and complete these factor trees
  a
  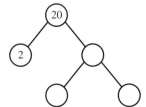

  b
  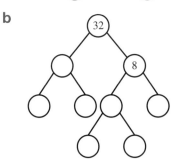

3 Write each of these numbers as the product of prime factors.
  a 12   **b** 18   **c** 26
  d 40   **e** 72   **f** 100

4 Use a calculator to find a prime factor greater than 10 for each of these numbers.
   a 169 **b** 255 **c** 176 **d** 322

5 Write 1920 as the product of its prime factors.

37.1 Exercise B

1 Write each product in index form
   a $2 \times 2 \times 3 \times 3 \times 3$
   b $3 \times 5 \times 5 \times 5 \times 5$
   c $2 \times 5 \times 5 \times 7 \times 7$
   d $3 \times 11 \times 11 \times 11 \times 17 \times 17$

2 Write each of these numbers as a product of its prime factors.
   Give your answer in index form.
   a 16 **b** 36 **c** 44
   d 81 **e** 96 **f** 200

3 Draw all the possible factor trees for 24

4 Write each of these numbers as a product of its prime factors.
   Give your answer in index form.
   a 300 **b** 500
   c 640 **d** 12 800

5 Is 3×5^4 the same as 15^4? Explain your answer.

37.2 Exercise A

1 For each of the following pairs of numbers
   i write down the factors of each number
   ii underline the common factors
   iii draw a circle around the highest common factor.
   a 12 and 14 **b** 15 and 35
   c 16 and 20 **d** 20 and 30
   e 21 and 42 **f** 25 and 55

2 Find the highest common factor (HCF) of the following sets of numbers
   a 8 and 14 **b** 14 and 21
   c 9 and 15 **d** 6, 18 and 24
   e 15, 25 and 40 **f** 12, 16 and 28

3 Find the highest common factor (HCF) of the following sets of numbers
   a 56 and 72
   b 55 and 105
   c 96 and 120
   d 18, 36 and 45
   e 48, 64 and 160
   f 75, 125 and 150

37.2 Exercise B

1 a Work out the highest common factor (HCF) of 45 and 60
   b Hence
      i simplify $\frac{45}{60}$
      ii factorise $45x + 60$

2 What is the HCF of all the multiples of 9?

3 What is the HCF of
   a $4x$, $6x$ and $10x$
   b $15xy$, $30xy$ and $35xy$?

4 The HCF of 28 and another number is 14 The other number is between 40 and 50 What is it?

5 The HCF of 45 and another number is 15 The other number has two digits. Write down all the possible values of the other number.

6 The HCF of two expressions is $8m$. One of the two expressions is $32m$. The other expression is smaller than $32m$. Write down all the possible expressions that the other expression could be.

37.3 Exercise A

1 Find the lowest common multiple (LCM) of each set of numbers.
   a 4 and 5 **b** 3 and 7
   c 6 and 10 **d** 5 and 7
   e 8 and 12 **f** 10 and 12
   g 3, 4 and 5 **h** 5, 7 and 10

2 Bob is a builder. He buys nuts and bolts. Nuts are sold in packets of 10. Bolts are sold in packets of 8

He wants to have the same number of each in stock.

  a What is the smallest number of nuts and bolts he can buy?

  b What is the least number of packets of each he should buy?

3 Find the LCM of each set of numbers.

  a 9 and 12   **b** 11 and 13

  c 15 and 25   **d** 14 and 20

  e 12 and 21   **f** 20 and 35

  g 9, 15 and 18   **h** 7, 15 and 20

4 A restaurant serves a set two-course meal for £35 or a set three-course meal for £40

One night the takings on two-course meals was exactly equal to the takings on three-course meals.

  a Find the lowest amount that the takings on two-course meals could have been.

  b Find the second lowest possible total takings.

37.3 Exercise B

1 Write each number as the product of its prime factors and use a diagram to work out the LCM of

  a 25 and 40   **b** 16 and 24

2 Here are the factors of 20

  1   2   4   5   10   20

What is the LCM of all the factors of 20?

3 **a** Find the LCM of the denominators of the fractions $\frac{1}{4}$ and $\frac{7}{10}$.

  b Write each fraction as an equivalent fraction with the LCM of 4 and 10 as the denominator.

  c Use your answers to part **b** to add the two fractions.

4 The least common multiple of 15 and another number is 60

The other number is below 30. What is it?

5 The least common multiple of 36 and another number is 540. Find the smallest number that it could be.

6 Dave says it is possible for the LCM of x and y to be bigger than xy.

Is Dave correct? Explain your answer.

Chapter 38

38.1 Exercise A

1 The grouped frequency distribution represents the length of 100 golf shots.

Length of shot, l (minutes)	Frequency, f	Midpoint, x	fx
$150 \leqslant l < 200$	7	175	1225
$200 \leqslant l < 250$	24		
$250 \leqslant l < 300$	60		
$300 \leqslant l < 350$	9		
	$\sum f =$		$\sum fx =$

  a Explain why the midpoint of the first group is 175

  b Copy and complete the table.

  c Find an estimate of the mean length of golf shot.

2 The table shows the weight of the biggest suitcase of 80 holidaymakers.

Weight, w, (kg)	Frequency, f
$10 \leqslant w < 14$	10
$14 \leqslant w < 18$	29
$18 \leqslant w < 22$	25
$22 \leqslant w < 26$	16

  a Copy the table. Add extra columns for the midpoint, x, of each group and for the value of fx. Complete these columns.

  b Hence find an estimate of the mean weight of suitcase.

3 The table shows the length of 50 episodes of a famous soap opera.

Length of episode, l, (minutes)	Frequency, f
$26 \leqslant l < 27$	18
$27 \leqslant l < 28$	15
$28 \leqslant l < 29$	12
$29 \leqslant l < 30$	5

Calculate an estimate of the mean length of an episode of this soap opera.

38.1 Exercise B

1 The weight of 100 plums is measured. The lightest plum is 8.4 g, the heaviest plum is 21.5 g.
The data is grouped into class intervals of length 5 g.
The first group is labelled $5 \leqslant w < 10$
Write down the labels for the rest of the groups.

2 The times taken for 30 horses to run around a race track are recorded to the nearest 0.1 seconds.

58.1	79.2	82.4	63.6	72.8
79.9	82.4	63.0	52.7	83.2
95.8	43.2	82.7	73.9	68.1
69.9	75.8	70.8	93.9	98.7
73.8	82.1	66.6	79.2	77.7
68.3	79.2	88.2	73.0	80.0

a Find the range of the times taken.
b Complete a grouped frequency distribution table using groups of width 10 seconds.
c Hence calculate an estimate of the mean time.
d Give **two** reasons why the value calculated in part **c** is an estimate.
e What is the percentage error caused by grouping the data and finding the estimate?
Comment on your answer.

3 Basil's rabbit has eaten some of his homework.

Time, t, (seconds)	Frequency, f
$20 \leqslant t < 30$	10
$30 \leqslant t < 35$	26
$35 \leqslant t < 40$	18
	1

The correct estimate of the mean for the table is 33 seconds.
Show that the missing label is $40 \leqslant t < 100$

38.2 Exercise A

1 The number of ice creams bought during a theatre show by a group of people is given in the table.

Number of ice creams	Frequency, f
0	5
1	11
2	6
3	3

Calculate the median number of ice creams bought by these people.

2 This frequency distribution shows Colin's scores for 15 rounds of golf.

Golf score (x)	Frequency, f
69	1
70	5
71	4
72	2
73	1
74	2

Calculate Colin's median score for a round of golf.

3 The frequency distribution shows the number of times per week that Janet goes swimming over the summer months.

Number of times	Frequency
1	7
2	3
3	1
4	1
5	1

Calculate the median number of times Janet goes swimming over a week.

4 The table shows the maximum daytime temperature each day in April.

Maximum daytime temperature (°C)	Frequency
15	3
16	4
17	2
18	10
19	3
20	8

Calculate the median daytime temperature in April.

38.2 Exercise B

1 Jarnail collects information from a police officer about the speeds of the first 30 cars going past his school. The data is in the form of the grouped frequency distribution below.

Speed (mph)	Frequency, f
$20 \leqslant x < 30$	21
$30 \leqslant x < 40$	6
$40 \leqslant x < 50$	3

a Find the group in which the median lies.
b Find the modal group.

2 The table shows the length of 50 episodes of a famous soap opera.

Length of episode, l, (minutes)	Frequency, f
$26 \leqslant l < 27$	18
$27 \leqslant l < 28$	15
$28 \leqslant l < 29$	12
$29 \leqslant l < 30$	5

a Write down the modal group.
b Find the group in which the median lies.

3 The table shows the weight of the biggest suitcase of 80 holidaymakers.

Weight, w, (kg)	Frequency
$10 \leqslant w < 14$	10
$14 \leqslant w < 18$	29
$18 \leqslant w < 22$	25
$22 \leqslant w < 26$	16

a Write down the modal group.
b Find the group in which the median lies.

4 The table shows the weight in grams of 59 apples.

Weight, w, (g)	Frequency
$20 \leqslant w < 40$	5
$40 \leqslant w < 60$	16
$60 \leqslant w < 65$	13
$65 \leqslant w < 70$	22
$70 \leqslant w < 100$	3

a Find the modal group.
b Find the group which contains the median.
c Some more apples, all over 70 g were collected.
How many more apples over 70 g would be required to change the group containing the median?

38.3 Exercise A

1 The grouped frequency distribution represents the length of 100 golf shots.

Length of shot, l, metres	Frequency, f
$150 \leqslant l < 200$	7
$200 \leqslant l < 250$	24
$250 \leqslant l < 300$	60
$300 \leqslant l < 350$	9

Draw a frequency polygon to represent this distribution.

2 The table shows the length of 50 episodes of a famous soap opera.

Length of episode, l, minutes	Frequency, f
$26 \leqslant l < 27$	18
$27 \leqslant l < 28$	15
$28 \leqslant l < 29$	12
$29 \leqslant l < 30$	5

Draw a frequency polygon to represent this distribution.

3 The table shows the weight of 60 bins full of rubbish.

Weight, w, (kg)	Frequency
$10 \leqslant w < 14$	7
$14 \leqslant w < 18$	21
$18 \leqslant w < 22$	20
$22 \leqslant w < 26$	12

Draw a frequency polygon to represent the data

38.3 Exercise B

1 The frequency polygon represents the time taken for 100 shoppers to complete their supermarket shopping one day.

Construct the grouped frequency distribution that corresponds to the frequency polygon.

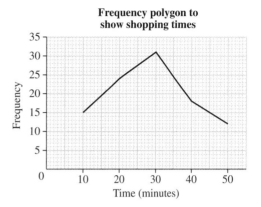

Frequency polygon to show shopping times

2 Estimate the mean time taken for the shoppers in question **1**

3 The frequency distribution shows the length, in centimetres, of 200 cucumbers entered in a biggest cucumber competition.

Length, l, (cm)	Frequency
$30 \leqslant l < 40$	$3t$
$40 \leqslant l < 45$	$5t$
$45 \leqslant l < 50$	$10t$
$50 \leqslant l < 65$	$2t$

a Find t.
b Draw the frequency polygon.
c Estimate the mean length of cucumber.

38.4 Exercise A

1 The table shows the weight of 60 bins full of rubbish.

Weight, w, (kg)	Frequency
$10 \leqslant w < 14$	7
$14 \leqslant w < 18$	21
$18 \leqslant w < 22$	20
$22 \leqslant w < 26$	12

Draw a histogram to represent the data.

2 The table shows the length of 50 episodes of a famous soap opera.

Length of episode, l, minutes	Frequency, f
$26 \leqslant l < 27$	18
$27 \leqslant l < 28$	15
$28 \leqslant l < 29$	12
$29 \leqslant l < 30$	5

Draw a histogram to represent this distribution.

3 The grouped frequency distribution represents the length of 100 golf shots.

Length of shot, l, metres	Frequency, f
$150 \leqslant l < 200$	7
$200 \leqslant l < 250$	24
$250 \leqslant l < 300$	60
$300 \leqslant l < 350$	9

Draw a frequency polygon to represent this distribution.

38.4 Exercise B

1 The histogram shows the speed of 100 balls bowled by a fast bowler in a test match.

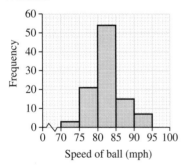

a What is the modal group?
b Calculate an estimate of the mean speed of a ball. Explain why the answer is only an estimate.
c Which group contains the median?
d Can you tell the speed of the fastest ball? Explain your answer.

2 Some students carried out a sponsored silence. Their results are shown by the frequency polygon.

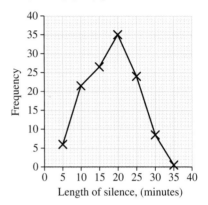

a How many students took part in the sponsored silence?
b Draw a histogram to illustrate the data.
c Estimate the mean number of minutes that a student stayed silent.
d Britney claimed she stayed silent for 41 minutes. Comment on Britney's claim.

3 Data was collected on the length of time passengers waited to get through the security check at the airport. 100 people were questioned, half waited under half an hour, 18 of these under 15 minutes. Of the rest (who waited over half an hour) only 9 waited more than 45 minutes and none over an hour.
Construct a histogram to show this data.

Chapter 39

39.1 Exercise A

1 a Draw and label a grid with the x-axis from -3 to $+3$ and the y-axis from -10 to $+10$
b Find the coordinates of the points that lie on the graph of $y = x + 6$ at $x = -2$, $x = 0$ and $x = 2$
c **i** On the grid draw and label the graph of $y = x + 6$
ii Work out the gradient of this line.

d Repeat parts **b** and **c** for

   i $y = x + 2$

   ii $y = x - 4$

   iii $y = x - 2$

   What do you notice about the gradient of each line?

e On a new copy of the same sized grid repeat parts **b** and **c** for

   i $y = 2x + 1$

   ii $y = -2x$

   iii $y = 4x - 3$

   iv $x + y = 7$

2 Draw a grid with the x-axis and y-axis from 0 to 13

  a **i** Find the value of y when $x = 0$ in $3x + y = 12$ and complete the coordinate (0, ...)

    ii Find the value of x when $y = 0$ in $3x + y = 12$ and complete the coordinate (..... , 0)

    iii On the grid draw the graph and label the graph $3x + y = 12$

  b Repeat part **a** for $5x + 2y = 12$

3 Graphs A to E are shown on the grid. Match each equation to its graph.

  Equation 1 $y = x$

  Equation 2 $y = -2x + 6$

  Equation 3 $y = -x + 5$

  Equation 4 $y = 4x - 3$

  Equation 5 $y = 3x + 2$

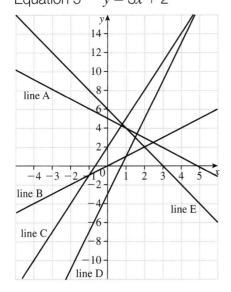

39.1 Exercise B

1 **a** Draw and label a grid with the x-axis from -3 to $+3$ and the y-axis from -10 to $+10$

  b On the grid draw and label the graph of $y = 4x - 1$

  c Use your graph to solve the following equations.

    i $4x - 1 = 3$ **ii** $4x - 1 = -9$

2 Draw and label a grid from 0 to 10 for both the x-axis and the y-axis.

Plot the points $A(4, 3)$, $B(5, 3)$ $C(4, 7)$ $D(4, 5)$ and $E(2, 9)$.

Which of the above points lie on the following lines?

  a $x = 4$ **b** $y = 3$

  c $x + y = 11$ **d** $y = x - 2$

  e $y = 2x - 3$ **f** $y = 3x + 1$

3 The time taken to cook large jacket potatoes in a microwave oven is given by

$$y = 3x + 5$$

where y is the time in minutes and x is the number of jacket potatoes.

  a Draw a grid with the x-axis from 0 to 12 and the y-axis from 0 to 40

  b On the grid draw the graph of $y = 3x + 5$

  c Use the graph to find the time to cook six potatoes.

  d It took 38 minutes to cook some potatoes. How many potatoes were cooked?

39.2 Exercise A

1 **a** Complete the table of values for $y = x^2 + 2x - 1$

x	-4	-3	-2	-1	0	1	2
y		2	-1	-2	-1		7

  b Draw the graph of $y = x^2 + 2x - 1$ for values of x from -4 to 2

  c Find the coordinates of the points where the line $y = 2$ crosses the graph of $y = x^2 + 2x - 1$

2 Draw all the graphs in this question on a grid with the x-axis from -4 to $+4$ and the y-axis from -10 to 14

  a Complete this table of values for $y = x^2 - 5$

x	-3	-2	-1	0	1	2	3
y							

  b On the grid draw and label the graph of $y = x^2 - 5$ for x from -3 to $+3$

  c Repeat **a** and **b** for
    i $y = x^2 + 3$ **ii** $y = x^2 - 1$

3 Draw all the graphs in this question on a grid with the x-axis from -4 to $+4$ and the y-axis from -40 to 40

  a Complete this table of values for $y = 4x^2$

x	-3	-2	-1	0	1	2	3
y							

  b On the grid draw and label the graph of $y = 4x^2$ for x from -3 to $+3$

  c Repeat **a** and **b** for
    i $y = -4x^2$ **ii** $y = 6 - x^2$
    iii $y = -3 - x^2$ **iv** $y = 2x^2 - 5$

4 Make a table of values and draw a graph using a suitable grid for each of the following quadratic functions.
  a $y = 2x^2 - 9$ for $x = -3$ to $+3$
  b $y = x^2 + 2x - 7$ for $x = -4$ to $+2$
  c $y = 3x^2 + 1$ for $x = -3$ to $+3$
  d $y = x^2 - 5x - 9$ for -2 to $+4$

39.2 Exercise B

1 Part of the graph of $y = x^2 - 3x + 2$ is shown on the grid.

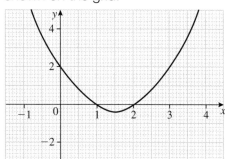

Use the graph to write down the solutions to $x^2 - 3x + 2 = 0$

2 Look at these sketches of quadratic equations.

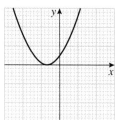

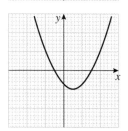

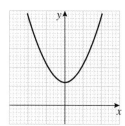

Which of the quadratic equations has
  a two solutions
  b exactly one solution
  c no solutions?

3 For each of the tables below
  a copy and complete the table
  b draw the graph of the quadratic
  c find the x-values for which the quadratic has y-value $= 0$
    i $y = 8 - 2x^2$

x	-3	-2	-1	0	1	2	3
y	-10		6		6		-10

    ii $y = (x - 3)(x - 5)$

x	1	2	3	4	5	6	7
y	8					3	

    iii $y = x^2 + 4x$

x	-5	-4	-3	-2	-1	0	1
y							

Chapter 40

40.1 Exercise A

1 *ABCD* is a rectangle.
   A is $(-3, 4)$, *B* $(5,4)$ and *C* $(5,1)$
   a Plot *A*, *B* and *C* on a grid
   b Plot the point *D* on the grid to
      complete the rectangle.
   c Write down the coordinates of *D*.

2 *W* $(2, 1)$, *X* $(2, 5)$, *Y* $(7, 4)$ and *Z* are the
   vertices of a parallelogram.
   Find two possible coordinates for *Z*.

3 Work out the midpoint of the line joining
   the points *R* $(-4, 5)$ and *S* $(2,10)$.

4 *A* is the point $(3,7)$.
   The midpoint of the line *AC* is the point *B*
   with coordinates $(9,10)$.
   Work out the coordinates of *C*.

5 Triangle *PQR* has vertices *P* $(10, 2)$,
   Q $(12, 6)$ and *R* $(16, 2)$.
   Work out the coordinates of the midpoint
   of each side of the triangle.

40.1 Exercise B

1
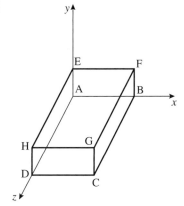

The diagram shows a cuboid drawn on a
3D grid.
A is the point $(0, 0, 0)$
F is the point $(6, 4, 0)$
G is the point $(6, 4, 11)$
Write down the 3D coordinates of
   a *B*   b *C*   c *D*   d *E*   e *H*

2 A cube *DEFGHIJK* has one vertex at
   $(0, 0, 0)$.
   Each edge has length two units. All the
   coordinates are zero or positive numbers.
   a Draw a sketch of the cube. Mark the
      x, *y* and *z*-axes clearly.
   b Write down the coordinate of each
      vertex *D* to *K*.

40.2 Exercise A

1 a Draw a line *AB* of length 9 cm.
   b Using ruler and compasses only,
      construct the perpendicular bisector
      of *AB*.

2 a Draw angle *ABC* such that *ABC* = 80°
   b Using ruler and compasses only,
      construct the bisector of angle *ABC*.

3 Using ruler and compasses only,
   a construct an equilateral triangle *XYZ*
      of side 5 cm
   b construct the bisector of angle *X* as
      far as the side *YZ*. Mark the point
      where the bisector meets *YZ* as *T*.
   c measure and write down the length *XT*.

4 Using ruler and compasses only,
   a construct triangle *LMN* with
      MN = 10 cm, *LM* = 8 cm and
      LN = 6.5 cm
   b construct the perpendicular bisector
      of *LM*
   c mark the point *P*, where the
      perpendicular bisector meets *MN*
   d measure and write down the distance
      from the midpoint of *LM* to *P*.

40.2 Exercise B

1 Make two copies of line *AB* where
   AB = 10 cm.
   a On the first copy, draw the locus of
      points that are
      i 4 cm from *A*   ii 7 cm from *B*
      iii shade the area which is less than
           4 cm from *A* and less than 7 cm
           from *B*.

b On the second copy draw the locus of points that are exactly 5 cm from AB. Shade the area which is less than 5 cm from AB.

2 A rectangle $ABCD$ has length $AB = 10$ cm and width $BC = 6$ cm.

  a Draw the rectangle.

  b Using ruler and compasses only, construct the locus of points equidistant from AB and AD and within 4 cm of A.

3 A ship is positioned 30 km from and due North of a lighthouse.

A small boat sends a distress signal.

It is within 10 km of the ship and within 25 km of the lighthouse.

Using ruler and compasses sketch the positions of the ship and lighthouse and shade the area which has to contain the boat.

Use a scale of 2 cm to represent 10 km.